The Best-Loved
PLAYS OF
SHAKESPEARE

BY JENNIFER MULHERIN AND ABIGAIL FROST

CHERRYTREE BOOKS

A Cherrytree book

Designed and produced by
A S Publishing
from titles first published by
Cherrytree Press Ltd in the
Shakespeare For Everyone
series
Reprinted 2007

This edition first published
by Cherrytree Books, part of the Evans Publishing Group
2A Portman Mansions
Chiltern St.
London W1U 6NR

British Library Cataloguing in Publication Data

Mulherin, Jennifer
     Best-loved Plays of Shakespeare
     1. Shakespeare, William. Macbeth
     I. Title II. Frost, Abigail
     822.33

     ISBN 1 84234 226 6
     13 - digit ISBN 978 1 84234 226 8

Typesetting by Dorchester Typesetting, Dorset
and Image Typographics, London

Printed in China through Colorcraft Ltd., Hong Kong

CONTENTS

INTRODUCTION
5

THE PLAYS

A MIDSUMMER NIGHT'S DREAM
11

THE MERCHANT OF VENICE
25

AS YOU LIKE IT
37

TWELFTH NIGHT
53

ROMEO AND JULIET
67

JULIUS CAESAR
83

MACBETH
97

HAMLET
113

KING LEAR
127

OTHELLO
143

THE LIFE AND PLAYS OF SHAKESPEARE
158

INDEX
159

The illustrations on the cover and on
pages 11, 25, 37, 53, 67, 83, 97 and 113 are
by Roger Payne; those on pages 127 and
143 are by Andrew Howat.

INTRODUCTION

The life of Shakespeare

Gent. Mag. July 1769.

R. Greene delin.
B. Cole sculp.

A House in Stratford upon Avon, in which the famous Poet Shakespear was Born.

William Shakespeare's birthplace in Henley Street, Stratford-upon-Avon. This illustration was made in 1769. The house still exists today and can be visited by the public.

The young Shakespeare

William Shakespeare's family had been humble farmers in Warwickshire since the Middle Ages. Then William's father decided to better himself and move to the town of Stratford, only a few miles from the family's home. John Shakespeare set up business as a glove maker, his work prospered and he was soon able to buy two houses in Henley Street, Stratford – and it was in one of these that Shakespeare was born in 1564.

Shakespeare's father had probably known his mother, Mary Arden, since childhood. Her father owned the land on which the Shakespeare family farmed. The Ardens lived in a large, comfortable house at Wilmcote (near Stratford) and were people of some standing in the district. They were regarded as minor gentry although they were not aristocratic or titled.

William was their third child – the two elder ones had died from plague – and altogether the Shakespeares had eight children. By the time William was old enough to go to school, his father's career had further prospered. He had become an alderman and bailiff (mayor) of the busy market town, and a justice of the peace.

Married at 18 years of age

It is almost certain that William went to the local grammar school where he would have been taught a good deal of Latin and some Greek. He would not have seen many plays in Stratford because in those days there were no public theatres. But strolling players sometimes visited country districts performing pageants; and occasionally miracle plays, where scenes from the Bible were acted out, were put on in Coventry, only 20 miles away. We do not know what Shakespeare did after he left school but one story says that he became a schoolmaster in the Cotswolds or in Lanca-shire. What we do know is that at the age of 18 he married Anne Hathaway, the daughter of a Stratford neighbour, who was eight years older than him. In 1583, his daughter Susanna was born and in 1585 the twins Hamnet and Judith. So by the age of 21, William had not only a wife but three children to support.

Stratford-upon-Avon in 1764. Both the church and the stone bridge are still standing. Shakespeare was baptized and buried in the church. And in a niche in the wall of the church, there is a bust of Shakespeare. This was placed there soon after his death.

Shakespeare becomes an actor in London

Why Shakespeare went to London and when is not certain. Most probably it was to earn some money, although one story relates that it was because he was caught poaching deer and rabbits on Sir Thomas Lucy's estate, Charlecote Park, near Stratford and forced to flee to the city. Whatever the reason, William came to London and became an actor.

From all accounts, Shakespeare was a good actor and he played both comic and tragic parts with different companies of actors. Life in the theatre was busy and, among humdrum

The Earl of Southampton,
Shakespeare's patron.
He was a rich young
nobleman of about
20 years of age when
Shakespeare met him.
Southampton encouraged
Shakespeare to write
poetry as well as plays.

things, William would have learned several actors' parts, because a new play was put on each day. He helped rewrite old plays and he was at this time trying his hand at writing plays himself. He toured different areas of the country with the company, he met fellow actors and played before the nobility and the court. So, in a fairly short while, he learned a good deal about life in the city and how it was lived by rich and poor alike – and about the government and the political events of the time.

Shakespeare in love

Unlike many writers at the beginning of their career, Shakespeare was lucky. His work attracted the attention of a young nobleman, the Earl of Southampton, who not only encouraged him to write poetry as well as plays but also introduced him to cultivated people who were interested in art, music, theatre and literature. It was at this time that he met and fell madly in love with the 'dark lady' of the *Sonnets* – a dark-haired, married woman who led him on, but in the end broke off their affair. Shakespeare's *Sonnets*, which contain some of the finest poetry written in the English language, express the joy and agony of that relationship.

Shakespeare the playwright

By about 1595 or 1596, Shakespeare was becoming well known as a writer of plays. He had already written some history plays, including *Richard III*, and also *The Taming of the Shrew* and *Romeo and Juliet*. In 1595, he became a shareholder in one of the most popular acting companies of the day. From then on, he spent the rest of his career writing plays for the company. After 1599 most were performed in the famous Globe Theatre on the south side of the Thames.

The theatre was one of the most popular kinds of entertainment in those days and Shakespeare wrote his plays for ordinary people. They loved his work and came again and again to see favourites, such as *Richard III* and *Macbeth*. The result was that he made quite a lot of money and was able to buy a large house, New Place, in Stratford. He also bought other property around Stratford. Because his father had been given a coat of arms earlier, Shakespeare was now regarded as a real gentleman and a man of standing – rather like his grandfather.

Shakespeare returns to Stratford

Shakespeare wrote over 35 plays and all of them were performed regularly, although some were more popular than others. In about 1610, Shakespeare left London and returned to Stratford to live; and after 1613 he wrote no more plays. We know almost nothing about his later life in Stratford. His beloved daughter, Susanna, who was married to a doctor, lived nearby and probably Shakespeare simply enjoyed his life, living in the company of his family – although he probably went to London from time to time.

Shakespeare died in 1616, some say from a fever he developed after a merry evening of eating and drinking with his friends, the poet Michael Drayton and the playwright Ben Jonson. In his will, Shakespeare left most of his possessions to Susanna and her husband and some small gifts to his best friends in the theatre company. He left the second best bed to his widow, not as an insult as many people think, but because it was almost certainly the bed they slept in – and because Susanna and her husband, or guests, might need the best one.

Anne Hathaway's cottage at Shottery near Stratford-upon-Avon. This thatched-roofed country dwelling belonged to the family of Shakespeare's wife, who were farmers. It still stands today.

A MIDSUMMER NIGHT'S DREAM

Illustrations by Norman Bancroft-Hunt

The story of A Midsummer Night's Dream

A royal wedding

In Athens, Theseus, Duke of the city, and Hippolyta his love, are to be married in four days' time on the night of the new moon on May 1. While they are discussing their plans, one of the Duke's citizens, Egeus, comes to him with a complaint. His daughter, Hermia, refuses to marry Demetrius, a young man approved of by her father, because she is in love with someone else.

Lovers' difficulties

The object of her affection is Lysander who, Egeus says, has won her over with compliments and gifts and made her disobedient to her father. The Duke points out that it is against the law in Athens to go against a father's wishes. He explains to Hermia that if she refuses to marry Demetrius, she will either be condemned to death or will have to spend the rest of her life as a nun in a convent – and he gives her four days until his wedding night to decide what she is going to do.

A plan to run away

As soon as Hermia and Lysander are alone together, he consoles her by telling her that 'the course of true love never did run smooth'. He thinks up a plan which will allow them to marry but it means running away to his aunt's house – some distance from Athens. Because of different laws in that part of the country, they can marry without Egeus's permission. The young lovers arrange to meet the next night in a wood near Athens and from there to make their escape.

Describing Hermia
Your eyes are lode-stars; and your tongue's sweet air
More tuneable than lark to shepherd's ear,
When wheat is green, when hawthorn buds appear.

Act I Sc i

How Helena betrays her friend

They tell their plan to Helena, Hermia's best friend from her schooldays. Helena has always been in love with

Demetrius and at one time he too was in love with her. She is unhappy and love-sick and she decides to tell Demetrius of the lovers' plan because, she thinks, he might then be kind and grateful to her. She knows that Demetrius will follow Hermia and Lysander to the woods, so she decides to follow him.

The tradesmen and their play

Meanwhile, all over Athens, events are being planned to celebrate the Duke's wedding. Among the ordinary folk of Athens, some tradesmen have arranged to put on a play for the Duke and his bride. The actors, who are all friends, are Quince, a carpenter, Snug, a joiner, Bottom, a weaver, Flute, a bellows mender, Snout, a tinker and Starveling, a tailor. These fellows do not know much about writing or

acting in plays. They have decided to write a play about the tragedy of two young lovers, Pyramus and Thisbe, but they cannot quite agree about who should play the different parts. So they arrange to meet by moonlight on the following night in a wood outside the town to go through the play without interruption.

Quarrel of Titania and Oberon

Now it is in this wood outside Athens that Oberon and Titania, the king and queen of the fairies, are to be found. They have come to Athens with their courtiers and attendants to honour the wedding of Theseus and Hippolyta. A mischievous goblin, Puck, is one of Oberon's attendants and we learn from him that Oberon and Titania have had a quarrel over a young Indian boy whom Titania has taken into her train but whom Oberon wants as his pageboy. Titania refuses to give the boy to her husband, so Oberon decides to play a trick on her. He sends Puck to find a magic flower whose juice can cast a spell over the person into whose eyes it is dropped. When the person wakes up, they fall in love with the first thing they see, whether it is an animal or a human being.

The love potion

While Oberon is hatching his plot, Demetrius comes into the wood in search of Hermia and Lysander – for it is now the following night when the lovers intend to escape He is angry because he is followed by the forlorn Helena who will not leave him alone, even though he keeps telling her that he does not love her. Oberon, who has overheard their conversation, feels sorry for Helena – and he decides that, as well as using the magic flower on Titania, he will also make Demetrius fall in love with Helena.

When Puck returns with the flower, Oberon takes some of it to put on Titania's eyes, while she sleeps nearby on a grassy bank. And he sends Puck to use it on Demetrius – who, Oberon tells him, is recognizable by his Athenian clothes. Oberon finds Titania being sung to sleep by her fairy train. When they leave her to sleep peacefully in her fairy bower, he squeezes the juices onto her eyelids.

Where Titania sleeps
I know a bank whereon the wild thyme blows,
Where oxlips and the nodding violet grows
Quite over-canopied with luscious woodbine,
With sweet musk-roses, and with eglantine:
There sleeps Titania some time of the night,
Lull'd in these flowers with dances and delight;

Act II Sc i

Puck's mistake

In the meantime, Hermia and Lysander have lost their way in the wood. They are weary and exhausted and decide to go to sleep for a little while – lying apart from each other out of modesty because they are not yet married. Moments after they have fallen asleep, Puck finds them and thinking that the young man in Athenian clothes must be Demetrius squeezes the juices into his eyes.

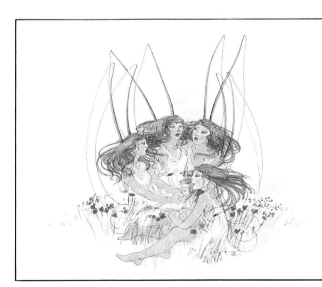

The fairies' song
You spotted snakes with double tongue,
*   Thorny hedge-hogs, be not seen;*
Newts and blind-worms, do no wrong:
*   Come not near our fairy queen.*
*   Philomel, with melody,*
*   Sing in our sweet lullaby;*
Lulla, lulla, lullaby; lulla, lulla, lullaby:
*   Never harm,*
*   Nor spell, nor charm,*
*   Come our lovely lady nigh,*
*   So, good night, with lullaby.*
Weaving spiders, come not here.

Act II Sc ii

A terrible mix-up

Demetrius, with Helena still following him, now arrives in this part of the wood but, in the darkness, he does not notice Hermia and Lysander asleep and he runs on. Helena, however, is tired and just as she decides to take a rest, she sees Lysander asleep and wakes him up. Because of the magic charm, he instantly falls in love with her – and to Helena's amazement, begins to declare his love with sweet words. Thinking that he is making fun of her, Helena becomes angry and leaves him in disgust – only to be followed by him. Hermia now wakes up from a bad dream and calls to Lysander but finds he has gone. Alarmed and afraid, she goes off in search of him.

Bottom turned into an ass

The rustic tradesmen now come into the wood to rehearse their play. By chance, they pick a spot close to where Titania lies asleep. As they talk about the play – Bottom is worried that the killings and lions in the story will upset the ladies – Puck comes upon them. Out of fun – for Puck is a naughty fellow – he decides to change Bottom into an ass. When his friends look up and see Bottom with the head of an ass, they become very alarmed and run away in fright. Bottom, unaware of how strange he looks, thinks he is being teased and that his friends are trying to frighten him.

Titania in love with an ass

Bottom sings a song to show how indifferent he is to being left alone but this awakens Titania. She immediately falls in love with him because of the magic flower that has been put in her eyes.

She leads him into her fairy bower and calls for her fairies, Pease Blossom, Cobweb, Moth and Mustard Seed, to attend to his every need.

In the meantime, Puck has returned to Oberon. He tells him that his trick has been successful – Titania has fallen in love with Bottom transformed into an ass and the young Athenian man has been given the love potion.

Demetrius has by this time found Hermia in the wood and he declares his love for her – but, as before, she refuses to accept him as a husband. Worried that some harm has come to Lysander, she goes off in search of him. Demetrius, by now exhausted, lets her go and he lies down to sleep.

Titania's instructions to her fairies
Be kind and courteous to this gentleman;
Hop in his walks, and gambol in his eyes;
Feed him with apricocks and dewberries,
With purple grapes, green figs, and mulberries.
The honey bags steal from the humble-bees,
And for night-tapers crop their waxen thighs,
And light them at the fiery glow-worm's eyes,
To have my love to bed – and to arise;
And pluck the wings from painted butterflies
To fan the moonbeams from his sleeping eyes:
Nod to him, elves, and do him courtesies.

Act III Sc i

Oberon's plan to sort out the mix-up

Oberon and Puck now arrive in this part of the wood. Oberon recognizes Demetrius at once and realises that Puck has mistakenly put the love potion in the eyes of the wrong young man. He at once sends Puck to find Helena and bring her back while he squeezes the magic juice into Demetrius's eyes. In that way when Demetrius wakes up

17

he will – as Oberon intended in the first place – fall in love with Helena.

More complications

Puck is saved the trouble of searching for Helena because at that moment she and Lysander appear. Lysander declares his love for her but she is still upset and thinks he is making fun of her. Demetrius now wakes up and since Helena is the first thing he sees, he declares his love in the most glowing and fulsome way. By now, Helena is very confused; she cannot understand why the two young men are in love with her, unless it is part of some joke they are playing just to humiliate her.

Hermia and Helena quarrel

Hermia now appears and is delighted at finding Lysander. When he swears that he is in love with Helena, Hermia thinks he is teasing. After a while she realises he is not. To her astonishment, both men are now in love, not with her, but with her schoolfriend. She gets into a rage, thinking that Helena has deliberately turned Lysander against her and that all three are making fun of her in a hurtful way. Helena, confused and unable to understand it all, believes that Hermia's outburst is further proof that the three are plotting against her. This leads to a terrible quarrel between the two girls, where they call each other names and even insult each other's appearance.

The two men also criticise Hermia and try to protect Helena from Hermia. Then they too begin to quarrel and go off into the forest to fight it out. Left alone with Hermia, Helena – who is a timid girl by nature – decides to run away, rather than have her eyes scratched out by Hermia.

Oberon makes it better again

The quarrel has been watched by Oberon and Puck. Puck thinks it has all been great fun but Oberon is cross that his plans have gone awry – and he orders Puck to put things right. He is to keep the young men apart, leading each one astray until they are so exhausted that they fall asleep in separate parts of the wood. He is then to use another magic potion on Lysander which destroys the effect of the love flower. This means that when Lysander wakes up, he will be in love with Hermia – as he really was before.

By this time, too, Hermia and Helena have gone their

separate ways but both are exhausted. All four lovers fall asleep in the wood. Unbeknownst to each other – because of the darkness – they are only a little distance apart.

Titania spellbound
Oberon in the meantime has gone off to find Titania to release her from the love spell. Bottom has been giving commands to the little fairies whom Titania has ordered to wait on him, but he becomes sleepy. Titania lovingly winds him in her arms and when Oberon arrives he finds this odd, ill-matched pair of lovers asleep. He uses a magic potion to release Titania from the love charm.

> **Titania with Bottom**
> *Come, sit upon this flow'ry bed,*
> *While I thy amiable cheeks do coy,*
> *And stick musk roses in thy sleek smooth head,*
> *And kiss thy fair large ears, my gentle joy.*

Act IV Sc i

Oberon and Titania reconciled
Oberon tells Puck, who has joined him, that he has made up his quarrel with Titania. She has agreed that he can have the Indian boy as his page. When Titania wakes up, she tells Oberon of her dream. When he points to Bottom lying beside her, she is filled with horror and disgust. Oberon tells Puck to take off the ass's head from the sleeping Bottom and the fairies go off to prepare for the Duke's wedding.

What the hunters find
As dawn breaks on May 1, Theseus, Hippolyta and members of the Athenian court set out from Athens on a hunting expedition. As they pass through the woods, they come upon the sleeping lovers. Thinking that they have arisen early to celebrate May 1, the Duke and his party wake them up.

Recounting the events of the midsummer night
Dazed and a little confused, the young lovers tell the Duke and Egeus, Hermia's father, about their reasons for being in the wood and the events of the past night. Demetrius, who is still under the magic spell, declares that he is really in

love with Helena. His passion for Hermia was just a passing thing. Lysander, of course, has also found that his love for Hermia has returned. The Duke is pleased that the lovers' difficulties have been sorted out; and he declares that their weddings will be celebrated with his own. Although the lovers are still uncertain about whether or not they are in a dream, they all go off to Athens to prepare for the wedding celebrations.

Bottom untransformed

Bottom, alone in the wood, now wakes up. He is just as dazed as the lovers, with vague memories of the attentions of Titania and the fairies. He goes home and calls at Quince's house, to find that his friends have been concerned about him. But Bottom has heard that their play is to be performed before the Duke that night; and he orders everybody to go off and get ready for it.

The 'tragedy' of Pyramus and Thisbe

The play is to be put on after the wedding ceremony and before the couples retire for the night. The Duke's master of ceremonies – who has seen the rustics rehearse – warns the Duke that the play is rather bad. The story of Pyramus and Thisbe is supposed to be a sad tale – but because the actors have never written or put on a play before, it turns out to be very funny. The tradesmen do not have any stage scenery, so they themselves act out not only the human characters but also other things which are in the play. These include a lion, a wall, the moon and a lantern. This makes it even more amusing – although, of course, the tradesmen did not mean it to be comic. Happily, the newly married couples are very pleased with their entertainment.

The fairies' blessing

When the play is over and the night draws to a close, the

The fairies' blessing

Through the house give glimmering light,
*   By the dead and drowsy fire:*
Every elf and fairy sprite
*   Hop as light as bird from brier;*
And this ditty, after me,
Sing and dance it trippingly.

Act v Sc ii

actors and spectators go off to bed. Then the fairies come into the palace. They are there to bless the marriages and the house, which they do by singing and dancing. When Oberon and Titania leave, Puck remains. He explains that, to many people, the story of *A Midsummer Night's Dream* may seem silly. But he cheerfully apologises and reminds us that dreams are often like that.

Puck's epilogue
If we shadows have offended,
Think but this, and all is mended:
That you have but slumber'd here,
While these visions did appear.
And this weak and idle theme,
No more yielding but a dream.

Act v Sc ii

21

Characters in A Midsummer Night's Dream

Hippolyta

Theseus

Amazons and after he had defeated them in battle he fell in love with their queen. In the play, Theseus is a wise and sensible man and a good ruler. Although he is sorry for Hermia because she is in love with Lysander, he will not allow her to disobey the laws of Athens. Later in the play, he is the person who talks common sense when the lovers tell the

story of their night in the woods. Although he is glad that their difficulties have been sorted out, he does not believe in dreams and fairy tales. These, he declares, only affect the brains of lovers and mad people. Real, everyday things are what he is concerned about.

He also shows that he is a kind man, and courteous and good-mannered to his subjects, as a good ruler should be. Theseus insists on seeing the Pyramus and Thisbe play. He knows that the humble folk have put a lot of effort into the play out of love and respect for their Duke. To Theseus, this is more important than whether the play is good or bad.

Hippolyta, too, is a fairly down-to-earth lady. She is fond of the open air and hunting and although she is a little puzzled by the midsummer night's events she, like Theseus, is glad that they have helped the lovers. Unlike her husband, she is bored by the play of Pyramus and Thisbe. 'This is the silliest stuff that I ever heard,' she says.

Theseus and Hippolyta

According to ancient Greek legend, Theseus was a great man who performed many brave deeds before he became ruler of Athens. Hippolyta, the lady whom he marries at the end of Shakespeare's play, was also a person of some importance, because she was the queen of a tribe of female warriors called the Amazons. According to ancient stories, Theseus went to war with the

Oberon and Titania

Oberon and Titania are king and queen of a fairy kingdom and we know that they have come to the wood near Athens from India (where they seem to live most of the time) in order to bless the marriage of Theseus and Hippolyta.

Because they are spirits, they have magical powers which, in this play, they use to help out the human beings. They are good fairies, unlike the witches in Shakespeare's play, *Macbeth*, who are evil. Oberon, for instance, uses the magic love juice to help the lovers with their problems and Titania and her fairies look after Bottom in a tender and thoughtful way.

Titania

These fairies do not live in the daytime, like ordinary people, but by night when they dance and sing by the light of the moon. When day breaks, they fly away to another land. In this play, Shakespeare links the fairies with all the beautiful things of nature. They describe the flowers and plants that grow in the wood and the creatures that live there. And they look after the flowers and blossoms, keeping away snakes and spiders. They use dewdrops to bless the royal house and they make crowns of flowers for Bottom. Most of the beautiful poetry in this play is spoken by them when they describe the natural things around them.

Hermia

Lysander

The young lovers
Shakespeare does not make Lysander and Demetrius, the two young Athenian men, really interesting people; he uses them more to show us what silly things people in love say and do. Demetrius is the more unkind of the two – he jilted Helena for Hermia and seems to care very little for poor Helena's feelings – while Lysander seems truly in love with Hermia, except when under the magic spell.

Shakespeare pays more attention to the girls. Helena is tall and fair and rather timid. For most of the play she is very

unhappy because, although she is in love with Demetrius, he is not in love with her. She also does not have a great deal of confidence in herself.

Hermia is short, dark and quick-tempered. When she thinks Helena has stolen Lysander away from her, she is furious and threatens to scratch out Helena's eyes. When

Helena

Demetrius

finally the lovers are woken up by Theseus, Demetrius, helped by the love juice, realises he is in love with Helena and Lysander regains his love for Hermia. The lovers are now happy – and like Bottom, they remember the events of the night but they are not sure whether they were a dream or not.

Oberon

Puck

Puck fetches the love potion
I'll put a girdle round about the earth
In forty minutes.

Act II Sc i

Puck

Puck is a different kind of fairy from Oberon and Titania. Although he plays the part of Oberon's servant and messenger, he is more like the goblins that appeared in fairy stories when Shakespeare was a boy. In the play, he is also called Robin Goodfellow and Hobgoblin and this character was a mischievous fellow, well known in many fairy tales for the pranks he played.

One of Titania's fairies recognizes him as the goblin who makes fun of people and Puck himself describes the jokes he often plays on ordinary village folk. Sometimes he upsets the dairymaids by skimming the cream from the milk or by getting in the dairy churn so that they cannot turn the cream into butter. On other occasions, he spoils beer which is being brewed, just for fun. Another favourite trick is to transform himself into a crabapple hidden inside a jug of ale. Then, when an old grandmother sips the ale, he bobs against her lips so that she spills it. His best 'joke', however, is to whip away a stool from an old lady as she is talking so that when she falls flat on the floor, everybody laughs.

Although he is a mischievous goblin, Puck is good and kind-hearted like the fairies. He goes ahead to clean the house before the fairies bless it (in the fairy stories of the time he often helped with the housework) and after they have flown away, he stays behind to talk to the audience who have been watching the play. Shakespeare lets Puck explain to us that the play is not meant to be very serious but that it is rather like a dream in which silly and improbable things can happen. If we have not enjoyed it, he says, he will try to make up for it with the next play we read or see – which will be better.

Bottom

Shakespeare intended Bottom and his fellow actors, the tradesmen, to be comic characters. They are funny, rather like clowns. And we laugh at them and their efforts to put on their play.

Nick Bottom is a weaver and he, along with his friends, is a simple, uneducated man like most of the ordinary citizens of Athens. Although we laugh at him, Bottom is a very likeable person. He is so keen about the play that he wants to play every part himself, describing for us how he would play each one in order to hold the audience's attention. 'Let me play the lion, too,' he says. 'I will roar, that I will do any man's heart good to hear me.'

Puck plays a trick on Bottom by turning him into an ass and Titania falls in love with him. Bottom seems to be rather amused by this and tells Titania that she has little reason for being in love with him. But he decides to go along with her infatuation and, like an actor in a play, he jokes and chats with Titania and the fairies, just as a true gentleman would.

Bottom

Bottom's instructions to the fairies
. . . help Cavalery Cobweb to scratch. I must to the
barber's, mounsieur; for methinks I am marvellous
hairy about the face; and I am such a tender ass, if
my hair do but tickle me, I must scratch.

Act IV Sc i

THE
MERCHANT OF VENICE

Illustrations by Norman Bancroft-Hunt

The story of The Merchant of Venice

Antonio, a merchant of Venice, is filled with a strange sadness. His friends think that he is worried about the ships he has abroad, in which he has put all his money. Antonio dismisses this idea and says he is simply sad by nature.

Antonio's sadness
I hold the world but as the world, Gratiano;
A stage where every man must play a part,
And mine a sad one.

Act i Sc i

Bassanio's problems
Bassanio is a handsome young nobleman who has fallen into debt. He explains that without money he cannot woo the beautiful heiress Portia whom he admires. Antonio, who loves his friend dearly, cannot lend Bassanio the money personally, but offers to borrow money for his friend from Shylock, the Jewish moneylender.

Portia and her suitors
Portia is rich and beautiful and lives on her estate at Belmont, a short distance away from Venice by sea. She is bored and discontented because she is not allowed to choose the husband she wants. In her father's will, he sets up a test for her suitors. They must choose between three caskets, one of silver, one of gold and one of lead. Only when they open the casket they have chosen will they – and Portia – know if they have won her hand in marriage. So far, she has not been very impressed with her suitors and speaks scathingly about them.

Portia describes one suitor
Nerissa *How like you the young German, the Duke of Saxony's nephew?*
Portia *Very vilely in the morning when he is sober, and most vilely in the afternoon, when he is drunk: when he is best, he is a little worse than a man, and when he is worst, he is little better than a beast*

Act i Sc ii

Shylock strikes a bargain
Shylock hates Antonio because he sometimes lends out money for nothing, while Shylock earns his living by lending money and charging interest. He is surprised when Antonio asks for a loan because Antonio has always spurned and abused him. Hatching a plot, Shylock agrees to lend 3000 ducats on one condition: if the debt is not paid, Shylock will demand one pound of Antonio's flesh 'cut off and taken in what part of your body pleaseth me.'

An exotic suitor for Portia

The most magnificent of Portia's suitors is the Prince of Morocco, who arrives at Belmont with courtiers all dressed in white. He hopes that Portia will not reject him because of his dark skin – but she, of course, has no choice in the matter. She leads him to the three caskets. Before he chooses, he must swear that, whatever the outcome, he will never court another woman.

Morocco's appeal to Portia

Mislike me not for my complexion,
The shadow'd livery of the burnish'd sun,
To whom I am a neighbour and near bred.
Bring me the fairest creature northward born,
Where Phoebus' fire scarce thaws the icicles,
And let us make incision for your love,
To prove whose blood is reddest, his or mine.

Act II Sci

A clown leaves his master

Back in Venice, Launcelot Gobbo, Shylock's clown, has decided to leave his master because of his miserliness. The poor but generous-hearted Bassanio agrees to take Launcelot into his service.

Gratiano, another young nobleman, pleads with Bassanio to be allowed to go to Belmont with him. Bassanio is reluctant because Gratiano is high-spirited and a chatterbox; he fears that Gratiano's talkative manner might upset people at Belmont, and ruin his chances with Portia. In the end, Bassanio is too soft-hearted to refuse his friend's request.

> **Bassanio on his friend's high spirits**
> *Thou art too wild, too rude and bold of voice;*
> *Parts that become thee happily enough,*
> *And in such eyes as ours appear not faults;*
> *But where thou art not known, why, there they show*
> *Something too liberal. Pray thee, take pain*
> *To allay with some cold drops of modesty*
> *Thy skipping spirit . . .*
>
> Act II Sc ii

Introducing Shylock's daughter, Jessica

Shylock's daughter, Jessica, bids farewell to Launcelot and gives him a message for her lover, Lorenzo. She asks him to rescue her from her father's house that night and promises to bring money and jewels.

Shylock is uneasy and reluctant to leave his house. He fears something is going to happen – 'For I did dream of moneybags tonight', he says. He knows that a masque (a theatrical entertainment) is to take place in Venice that night and he warns Jessica to keep the house locked up.

> **Shylock's instructions to Jessica**
> *Lock up my doors; and when you hear the drum,*
> *And the vile squealing of the wry-neck'd fife,*
> *Clamber not you up to the casements then,*
> *Nor thrust your head into the public street*
> *To gaze on Christian fools with varnish'd faces,*
>
> Act II Sc iv

Exit Jessica with the jewels

As promised, Lorenzo and his friends wait outside Shylock's house. They are dressed for the masque so that their faces are hidden. When Jessica appears at the window, she throws down a casket containing jewels and money. She herself follows, dressed in boy's clothes; it has been arranged that she will pretend to be Lorenzo's torch-bearer. Lorenzo declares his love for this brave girl.

Lorenzo declares his love for Jessica
Beshrew me, but I love her heartily;
For she is wise, if I can judge of her,
And fair she is, if that mine eyes be true,
And true she is, as she hath prov'd herself;
And therefore, like herself, wise, fair, and true,
Shall she be placed in my constant soul.   Act II Sc vi

Morocco chooses the casket

Back in Belmont, the Prince of Morocco is about to choose the casket. Each one has an inscription which he reads. If he chooses the right one, it will contain a portrait of Portia.

> **The inscriptions on the caskets**   Act II Sc vii
> *This first, of gold, which this inscription bears:*
> Who chooseth me shall gain what many men desire.
> *The second, silver, which this promise carries:*
> Who chooseth me shall get as much as he deserves.
> *This third, dull lead, with warning all as blunt:*
> Who chooseth me must give and hazard all he hath.

The prince chooses the gold casket because he believes that all the world must desire Portia. Alas, when he opens it, it contains a skull with a message.

> **The golden casket's message**
> *All that glisters is not gold;*   *Had you been as wise as bold,*
> *Often have you heard that told:*   *Young in limbs, in judgment old,*
> *Many a man his life hath sold*   *Your answer had not been inscroll'd, –*
> *But my outside to behold:*   *Fare you well; your suit is cold.*
> *Gilded tombs do worm infold.*
>   Act II Sc vii

The Prince has failed and he leaves, grieved and disappointed.

Bassanio makes his way to Belmont

Bassanio with Gratiano sets sails for Belmont while another suitor, the Prince of Arragon, takes his chances with the casket. A conceited man, he chooses the silver casket, but finds only a fool's head when he opens it.

Disastrous news in Venice

In Venice, news has spread that Antonio has lost one of his most valuable ships. Shylock vows he will now extract his

> **Shylock's reason for revenge**
> *He hath disgraced me, and hindered me half a million, laughed at my losses, mocked at my gains, scorned my nation, thwarted my bargains, cooled my friends, heated mine enemies; and what's his reason? I am a Jew. Hath not a Jew eyes? hath not a Jew hands, organs, dimensions, senses, affections, passions? fed with the same food, hurt with the same weapons, subject to the same diseases, healed by the same means, warmed and cooled by the same winter and summer, as a Christian is? If you prick us, do we not bleed? if you tickle us, do we not laugh? if you poison us, do we not die? and if you wrong us, shall we not revenge? If we are like you in the rest, we will resemble you in that.*
>   Act III Sc i

pound of flesh. He is driven by revenge because Antonio has always hated him for being a Jew.

Shylock is more concerned by the loss of his money than by the loss of his daughter. He hears, too, that she has wasted his money, even selling a ring which had sentimental value for him.

Bassanio chooses a casket

Portia is reluctant for Bassanio to choose the casket. She has fallen in love with him and fears that he will fail the test – but Bassanio is impatient to know his fate. As he goes to the caskets, Portia instructs her musicians to play sweet music. Bassanio chooses the lead casket, opens it and finds Portia's portrait. Portia humbly offers herself and all her worldly goods to him and gives him a ring as a love token. Bassanio can hardly believe his fortune.

Portia's acceptance
You see me, Lord Bassanio, where I stand,
Such as I am . . . but the full sum of me
Is sum of nothing; which, to term in gross,
Is an unlesson'd girl, unschool'd, unpractis'd;
Happy in this, she is not yet so old
But she may learn; happier than this,
She is not bred so dull but she can learn;
Happiest of all is that her gentle spirit
Commits itself to yours to be directed,
As from her lord, her governor, her king.
Myself and what is mine to you and yours
Is now converted . . . .

Act III Sc ii

To the couple's surprise and delight, Nerissa, Portia's lady-in-waiting, announces that she and Gratiano have fallen in love.

News of Antonio

Their happiness is interrupted when news arrives of Antonio's troubles; he is to appear in court before the Duke of Venice. Bassanio departs immediately to be with his friend, while Nerissa and Portia make plans to go to a nearby monastery to await the return of the men. In fact, Portia has quite different ideas. She intends to go to Venice dressed as a young lawyer to defend Antonio. She leaves the care of her house in Belmont to Lorenzo and Jessica.

In the Venetian courtroom

Antonio knows that the Duke of Venice cannot help him because the bond is a legal one, and the law must be upheld. He prepares to meet his fate.

In the courtroom, the Duke tries to reason with Shylock. Bassanio offers double the bond money but Shylock will not be moved.

Antonio on his fate

I am a tainted wether of the flock,
Meetest for death: the weakest kind of fruit
Drops earliest to the ground; and so let me:
You cannot better be employ'd, Bassanio,
Than to live still, and write mine epitaph.

Act IV Sc i

Enter the young 'doctor of law'

Just then, Portia, dressed as a young lawyer, arrives with her 'clerk', Nerissa. She informs the court that she has been sent by Dr. Bellario from Padua to fight the case. She admits that Shylock has the law on his side, but asks him to be merciful.

Portia's plea for mercy

The quality of mercy is not strain'd,
It droppeth as the gentle rain from heaven
Upon the place beneath: it is twice bless'd;
It blesseth him that gives, and him that takes:
'Tis mightiest in the mightiest; it becomes
The throned monarch better than his crown;
His sceptre shows the force of temporal power,
The attribute to awe and majesty,
Wherein doth sit the dread and fear of kings;
But mercy is above this sceptred sway,
It is enthroned in the hearts of kings,
It is an attribute to God himself,
And earthly power doth then show likest God's
When mercy seasons justice.

Act IV Sc i

How Shylock is defeated

Portia then utters a warning. In taking the pound of flesh, Shylock must not shed 'one drop of Christian blood' – otherwise, all his property will be confiscated. Shylock realizes he cannot win; he is defeated. Although the Duke allows him to live, Shylock leaves the court a broken man.

A gift for the lawyer

The young lawyer refuses a gift of money, but presses Bassanio for the ring given to him by Portia. Reluctantly, he parts with it, as does Gratiano with his, which goes to the lawyer's clerk.

Harmony – and disharmony – in Belmont

As Lorenzo and Jessica linger at night in the garden at
Belmont, he describes the power of music. Soon after, Nerissa
and Portia arrive home, followed by Bassanio, Gratiano and
Antonio. Portia makes Antonio most welcome, but then a
quarrel breaks out between the young couples over the loss of
the wedding rings. Portia pretends to be very angry – but
then reveals that she has the ring, explaining, to the men's
amazement, that she and Nerissa were the lawyer and his
clerk. News arrives that Antonio's ships have arrived safely
at port, and the joy of everyone is complete.

Characters in The Merchant of Venice

In Portia's praise
In Belmont is a lady richly left,
And she is fair, and, fairer than that word,
Of wondrous virtues: sometimes from her eyes
I did receive fair speechless messages:
Her name is Portia.

Act I Sc i

Portia

Shylock

Why Shylock hates Antonio
Signior Antonio, many a time and oft
In the Rialto you have rated me
About my moneys and my usances . . .
You call me misbeliever, cut-throat dog,
And spet upon my Jewish gaberdine,
And all for use of that which is mine own.

Act I Sc iii

Portia

Portia is very beautiful and extremely rich, and suitors come from 'the four corners of the earth' to woo her. At the beginning of the play, she is rather bored and dissatisfied, but after she is won by Bassanio her real personality emerges. Intelligent and quick-witted, she decides to help Antonio, and as a result of her cleverness in the courtroom she saves the day. She is a very capable lady, and generous with both her love and her money. Bassanio is especially fortunate to have won such a prize.

Shylock

Thou call'dst me dog before thou hadst a cause, But, since I am a dog, beware my fangs.

Shylock is the best-known character in this play. He is a forceful but villainous person who is driven by hate and greed. Although he has many reasons to hate Antonio, who spurns him because he is Jewish, his desire for revenge is fuelled by great bitterness and anger. He is a man who has no warmth or love in him, not even for his own daughter. He displays little human feeling of any kind except when he talks with passion about his treatment as a Jew.

Antonio

In sooth, I know not why I am so sad: It wearies me; you say it wearies you;

Although the play is named after him, Antonio plays a fairly small part in the play. He seems a rather sad figure because, although he has close friends like Bassanio, he has no wife or lover. His kindness and generosity to his young friend is

Antonio

Lorenzo talks of love

The moon shines bright: in such a night as this,
When the sweet wind did gently kiss the trees
And they did make no noise, in such a night
Troilus methinks mounted the Troyan walls,
And sigh'd his soul toward the Grecian tents,
Where Cressid lay that night.

Act v Sci

Bassanio

Jessica

There is more difference between
thy (Shylock's) *flesh and hers*
than between jet and ivory.

Jessica shares none of her
father's characteristics. She is
young and pretty with a sense of
fun, and she is rather impulsive.
Although we cannot blame her
for eloping with Lorenzo, we
feel uneasy about her stealing
her father's money and jewels –
especially when she spends the
money so extravagantly. Her
sunny, open nature, however,
is very winning, and since
Shakespeare sympathises with
her we do, too.

boundless. He is, without
doubt, the most noble and
unselfish person in the entire
play, and in the end gets his just
reward.

Bassanio
Although Bassanio is a
handsome young man who is
chivalrous, sociable and
generous-spirited, many people
have criticised him for being a
fortune hunter and a
spendthrift. He seems to have
no money of his own, although
he has an extravagant lifestyle.
He relies, first, on the
generosity of Antonio, who
borrows money for him; after
he has won Portia, it is her
money which will pay his debts.
This would not have worried
the Elizabethans who knew of
many young noblemen who
lived beyond their means.
Bassanio is a true gentleman
and a loving friend to Antonio;
and his warmth and honesty
make him a worthy hero.

Lorenzo
Lorenzo is a handsome, dashing
young man. Having fallen in
love with Jessica, he rescues her
and elopes with her. His easy
and friendly ways are valued by
Portia, who leaves the couple in
charge of her house at Belmont.
Lorenzo's conversations with
Jessica are full of lovely poetry
and playfulness; they are a
couple whom we feel sure will
live happily ever after.

Lorenzo

Jessica

AS YOU LIKE IT

Illustrations by George Thompson

The story of As You Like It

Orlando is badly treated by his elder brother, Oliver. He tells Adam, their dead father's old servant, that Oliver will not give him the money left to him by their father. Instead, he makes him work like a poor peasant.

Oliver plots against his brother
Oliver and Orlando quarrel and Oliver decides on revenge against his brother. He arranges a wrestling match between the champion, Charles, and his brother. Charles is instructed to kill Orlando.

The banished Duke
Meanwhile at court, the old Duke has been banished by his younger brother, Duke Frederick, who now rules the land. The old Duke and his followers have fled to the Forest of Arden where they live in peace and harmony. Rosalind is the old Duke's daughter but she has been allowed to stay at court because she is the greatest friend of Celia, Duke Frederick's daughter.

The wrestling match
The court has gathered to watch the wrestling match between Orlando and Charles. Rosalind has fallen in love with Orlando at first sight and she begs him not to fight. Orlando insists, saying it does not matter if he dies.

> **Orlando before the wrestling match**
> *I shall do my friends no wrong, for I have none to lament me; the world no injury, for in it I have nothing . . .*
>
> Act I Sc ii

In fact, Orlando throws Charles and wins the wrestling match. Rosalind is delighted and gives him a locket. When Duke Frederick learns that Orlando is the son of an enemy, he is displeased and he dismisses him.

Rosalind is banished
Rosalind confesses to Celia that she has fallen in love with Orlando. They are disturbed by Celia's father who angrily

39

accuses Rosalind of being a traitor. He orders her to leave the kingdom. Celia asks the Duke for a reason but he merely points out how much people admire Rosalind.

> **Why Rosalind must leave**
> *She is too subtle for thee; and her smoothness,*
> *Her very silence and her patience,*
> *Speak to the people, and they pity her.*
> *Thou art a fool: she robs thee of thy name ...*
>
> Act I Sc iii

Celia declares she will go into exile with Rosalind. The two decide to seek out Rosalind's father in the Forest of Arden. Disguised as a young man called Ganymede, Rosalind will accompany a 'sister', Celia. Touchstone, the court jester, agrees to go with them.

Meanwhile, in the Forest of Arden, the old Duke and his followers muse on how pleasant their simple life is compared to that at court.

> **The pleasures of country life**
> *And this our life exempt from public haunt,*
> *Finds tongues in trees, books in the running brooks,*
> *Sermons in stones, and good in every thing.*
>
> Act II Sc i

Back at Oliver's house, Orlando learns from Adam that his brother plans another attempt on his life. He decides to flee, and Adam begs to go with him. When Adam offers Orlando all his money, the young man is touched. Together, they go off to seek their fortune.

> **Orlando expresses his gratitude**
> *O good old man! how well in thee appears*
> *The constant service of the antique world,*
> *When service sweat for duty, not for meed!*
>
> Act II Sc iii

In the Forest of Arden

Celia, Rosalind and Touchstone at last arrive in the Forest of Arden. They are so weary they can go no further. By chance, they overhear a young shepherd, Silvius, talking to an older man, Corin, about his love for a shepherdess called Phebe. They ask Corin where they can get food and shelter. He leads

them to a sheep farm which is for sale. They like it and decide to buy it.

At the old Duke's encampment
Orlando and Adam arrive in the Forest of Arden but Adam is too weak from hunger to go on. Orlando goes in search of food. Meanwhile, the Duke's followers are singing a song.

A country song

Under the greenwood tree
Who loves to lie with me,
And turn his merry note
Unto the sweet bird's throat,
Come hither, come hither, come hither:
Here shall he see
No enemy
But winter and rough weather.

Act II Sc v

Orlando comes upon the Duke's encampment. He threatens to kill everyone unless he is given food. The Duke answers him politely and offers his hospitality. Orlando apologises for being rude and goes to fetch Adam. Jaques, a melancholy nobleman, talks about the life of man. He says it is rather like a stage play with seven different acts.

> **Seven ages of man**
> *All the world's a stage,*
> *And all the men and women merely players:*
> *They have their exits and their entrances;*
> *And one man in his time plays many parts,*
> *His acts being seven ages. At first the infant,*
> *Mewling and puking in the nurse's arms . . .*
> *. . .And then the lover,*
> *Sighing like furnace, with a woful ballad*
> *Made to his mistress' eyebrow . . . Last scene of all,*
> *That ends this strange eventful history,*
> *Is second childishness and mere oblivion,*
> *Sans teeth, sans eyes, sans taste, sans everything.*
>
> 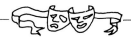 Act II Sc vii

Back at court, Duke Frederick questions Oliver about his brother's disappearance. He orders him to find Orlando and bring him back, dead or alive.

In praise of Rosalind

Orlando hangs verses in praise of Rosalind on trees in the forest. They are found by both Rosalind and Celia. Celia, who has seen Orlando in the forest, reveals that the verses are his. Just as Rosalind is eagerly questioning her friend, Orlando arrives. Rosalind, dressed as Ganymede, approaches him. She talks to him about love and offers to cure his lovesickness by pretending to be his Rosalind – whom he must woo.

> **Rosalind's views on love**
> *Love is merely a madness, and, I tell you, deserves*
> *as well a dark house and a whip as madmen do.*
> Act III Sc ii
>
>

Orlando does not want to be cured of love but he likes talking to Ganymede. He agrees to take her cure.

The jester in love

Meanwhile, Touchstone has fallen in love with Audrey, a simple country girl who tends goats. He has arranged to be married to her by a local vicar in the forest. Jaques, who has overheard their talk, tells Touchstone to get married properly in a church.

'The proud disdainful shepherdess'
Silvius, the young shepherd, is having no luck in winning the love of Phebe. Celia and Rosalind watch unnoticed as she scorns his love in a cruel way. Rosalind steps forward and rebukes Phebe for rejecting Silvius.

Rosalind's rebuke

But, mistress, know yourself: down on your knees,
And thank heaven, fasting, for a good man's love:
For I must tell you friendly in your ear,
Sell when you can; you are not for all markets.

Act III Sc v

The wooing of Rosalind
As arranged, Orlando visits Rosalind for his love 'cure'. 'Come, woo me, woo me; for now I am in a holiday humour, and like enough to consent,' she says. Orlando says he would die for love of Rosalind but 'Ganymede' scoffs at this romantic idea.

Orlando soon has to hurry away to keep an appointment.
Rosalind eagerly awaits his return in a couple of hours.

Meanwhile, Silvius delivers a letter from Phebe to
Rosalind. He is unaware of its contents but Phebe has fallen
in love with 'Ganymede'. It is a love letter.

Enter Oliver

Just then Oliver arrives looking for Celia and Rosalind. He
tells that he was sleeping in the forest and that a lioness was
ready to pounce on him. He was rescued by Orlando but in
the struggle Orlando was wounded by the beast. Overcome
with gratitude and love, Oliver tells how he has become
reunited with his brother.

He carries Orlando's bloodstained handkerchief, and a
message for the youth 'Rosalind' – Orlando cannot keep his
appointment. So alarming is this news that Rosalind faints,
but she quickly pretends she is only play-acting. She is weak
and pale, though, and has to be helped back to the cottage.

Audrey's suitor dismissed

Audrey complains to Touchstone about not being married yet. He asks her to be patient. Just then, a young country boy, William, arrives. He is interested in courting Audrey. Touchstone talks to him, showing off his clever, courtly ways. He threatens him and then sends him on his way in no uncertain terms.

> ### Touchstone's dismissal of William
> *. . . abandon the society of this female, or, clown, thou perishest; or to thy better understanding, diest; or, to wit, I kill thee, make thee away, translate thy life into death, thy liberty into bondage.*
>
> Act v Sc i

Love at first sight

Oliver tells Orlando that he and Celia have fallen in love and intend to marry. He bequeaths his inheritance to Orlando, declaring that he intends to lead the life of a shepherd in the forest. Orlando and Rosalind discuss the good news. She explains that it was love at first sight.

> ### Love explained
> *. . . for your brother and my sister no sooner met, but they looked; no sooner looked but they loved; no sooner loved but they sighed; no sooner sighed but they asked one another the reason.*
>
> Act v Sc ii

Orlando wishes that he too could be married to his Rosalind. Rosalind reveals that she has magic powers and can make this happen. Phebe and Silvius arrive. Although he is still in love with Phebe, she wants to marry Ganymede. Rosalind promises that all their wishes will be fulfilled the following day.

> ### What love is
> *It is to be all made of fantasy,*
> *All made of passion, and all made of wishes;*
> *All adoration, duty and observance;*
> *All humbleness, all patience, and impatience;*
> *All purity, all trial, all obeisance.*
>
> Act v Sc ii

A joyful day

Touchstone and Audrey too are looking forward to the following day when they are to be married. Two of the Duke's pages sing them a charming love song.

A love song
It was a lover and his lass,
  With a hey, and a ho, and a hey nonino,
That o'er the green corn-field did pass,
  In the spring time, the only pretty ring time,
When birds do sing, hey ding a ding, ding;
Sweet lovers love the spring.

Act v Sc ii

Rosalind's promises

On the day when Rosalind's promises are to be fulfilled, she

explains to the old Duke exactly what they are. If his daughter, Rosalind, appears she will be given in marriage to Orlando. The Duke agrees to this, as does Orlando. Phebe promises that she will marry Ganymede – but, if she changes her mind, she agrees to marry Silvius. Celia and Rosalind then leave to prepare for the celebrations.

Touchstone and Audrey arrive. Jaques recognizes him as the jester he has often seen in the forest. Having spoken to Touchstone, he knows that the jester has lived at court. Touchstone amuses the company with his talk of how a courtier behaves. He asks if he and Audrey can be married with the other couples.

The courtier, Touchstone
... I have trod a measure; I have flattered a lady; I have been politic with my friend, smooth with mine enemy; I have undone three tailors ...

Act v Sc iv

Celia and Rosalind arrive dressed in court clothes. The god of marriage arrives to bestow a solemn blessing on the couples.

The promises fulfilled
All the puzzles are now solved. Orlando realises that the young man he has wooed is his beloved Rosalind. Phebe now knows that Ganymede is a girl and agrees to marry Silvius.

Just then Jaques, the youngest brother of Orlando and Oliver, arrives with important news. Celia's father, who had set out to confront the old Duke in the forest, has been converted to a religious life. He met a hermit on the way and has given his crown and lands to the old Duke. The melancholy Jaques, who believes that he can learn much by taking up a religious life, decides to join Duke Frederick. The rest of the company prepare to celebrate the young couples' marriages.

Rosalind's epilogue
The play is over and Rosalind comes on to the stage to talk to the audience. She jokes with them, saying that a good play should not need an epilogue. She asks the men and women in turn to approve of the play. She then curtsies and bids the audience farewell.

Characters in As You Like It

Rosalind

*From the east to western
    Ind,
No jewel is like Rosalind.*

Rosalind is one of the most charming of all Shakespeare's female characters. She is bright, witty and able to talk and joke with everyone. She is at her most attractive in the wooing game she plays with Orlando. Although she flirts with him, she also talks a lot of common sense. Even though she is dressed as a boy, she behaves with girlish feelings. She faints, for instance, when she hears that Orlando has been wounded. She has, however, to use her imagination to solve the problems created by her Ganymede identity.

Orlando

*I will chide no breather in
    the world but myself,
against whom I know
    most faults.*

Brave, strong and handsome, Orlando seems a worthy lover for any young woman. He has a generous, kind nature which shows in the care he takes of Adam. Although he has been badly treated by his brother, he nobly rescues him from the lioness. He is a true gentleman despite his life as a peasant; he apologises to the gentle Duke for his impolite behaviour. His verses to Rosalind show him to be romantic. However, in the wooing game with Rosalind, she does seem to out-talk him with her witty comments.

Rosalind

Orlando

Rosalind in love
*. . . I will be more jealous of thee than a Barbary
cock-pigeon over his hen; more clamorous than a parrot
against rain; more new-fangled than an ape; more giddy in
my desires than a monkey . . .*

Act IV Sc i

Oliver's nature

O! I have heard him speak of that same brother;
And he did render him the most unnatural
That liv'd 'mongst men.   Act IV Sc iii

Oliver

Celia

Celia

Celia is Rosalind's dearest friend and the two girls are as close as sisters. Celia's great quality is her loyalty to her friend. When Rosalind is banished by Duke Frederick, Celia chooses to go with her. This is not only because she loves her friend but also because she believes her father is wrong in calling Rosalind a traitor. Like Rosalind, she is witty and amusing. She teases Rosalind about being in love with Orlando and about his verses. Although she warns Rosalind against love at first sight, she falls instantly in love with Oliver. Her warm and generous nature make her very appealing and the audience knows that she will make the perfect wife – even as a shepherdess.

Oliver

At the beginning of the play, Oliver is a villain. Not only does he treat his brother with contempt, he also wants to kill him. He is jealous of Orlando's good nature and popularity. When the wrestler fails to kill Orlando as planned, Oliver makes another attempt. It is hard to believe that such a character can have a complete change of heart, but he does. After his rescue by Orlando, his good qualities emerge.

A close friendship

. . . we still have slept together,
Rose at an instant, learn'd, play'd, eat together;
And whereso'er we went, like Juno's swans,
Still we went coupled and inseparable.
                                              Act I Sc iii

Melancholy Jaques

... it is a melancholy of mine own, compounded of many simples, extracted from many objects, and indeed the sundry contemplation of my travels, which, by often rumination, wraps me in a most humorous sadness.

Act IV Sc i

Jaques

I can suck melancholy out of a song as a weasel sucks eggs.

Jaques is one of the old Duke's followers. He is a melancholy person who is always thinking and talking about the meaning of life. When a deer is slaughtered he weeps in sympathy with the animal. He sees a moral in almost everything that happens. And he is also clever and wise about the ways of the world. In the play his main purpose is to comment on the actions of the other characters.

Touchstone

Touchstone is a court jester. He earns his living by playing the fool and amusing people. He makes fun of Orlando's love verses and jokes about country ways and court manners. He brings people down to earth with his clever comments. He marries Audrey but unlike the other lovers, he hopes to get out of it afterwards.

Touchstone on his beloved

A poor virgin sir, an ill-favoured thing, sir, but mine own

Act v Sc iv

Audrey

Audrey is an ordinary country girl who looks after goats. She is not very clever but she has an honest, simple nature which is why Touchstone likes her. And she is probably flattered to find favour with such a worldly man. She is not a make-believe country person, but a real one.

Jaques   Audrey   Touchstone

A fool's life

He uses his folly like a stalking-horse, and under the presentation of that he shoots his wit.

Act v Sc iv

TWELFTH NIGHT

Illustrations by George Thompson

The story of Twelfth Night

> *If music be the food of love, play on,*
> *Give me excess of it, that, surfeiting,*
> *The appetite may sicken, and so die.*
> *That strain again, it had a dying fall:*
> *O, it came o'er my ear like the sweet sound*
> *That breathes upon a bank of violets,*
> *Stealing and giving odour. Enough, no more;*
> *'Tis not so sweet now as it was before.*

Act I Sc i

Orsino, Duke of Illyria, listens to music and talks about love. He is melancholy because he is in love with a noble lady, Countess Olivia, but she has rejected his love. She is determined not to marry because she is in mourning after the death of her beloved brother.

A shipwreck

Meanwhile on the coast of Illyria, a young girl, Viola, has been shipwrecked with the ship's captain and some sailors. She fears that her twin brother, Sebastian, has been drowned. The captain comforts her, saying he believes Sebastian may have survived. He tells Viola about the Duke's love for Olivia, and how Olivia will not receive any visitors or messages because she is in mourning. Viola realizes that it is not possible for her to become one of Olivia's ladies-in-waiting, as she had planned. So instead, she decides to dress as a pageboy and join Orsino's household; she knows that he is fond of music and she can sing and play musical instruments.

Introducing Sir Toby Belch

Olivia has an older cousin, Sir Toby Belch, who lives in her household. He likes to spend his time drinking and merrymaking. But with Olivia now in seclusion, he complains to Maria, Olivia's lady-in-waiting, that this restricts his fun. Sir Toby has a particular friend, Sir Andrew Aguecheek, whom he invites to stay. Sir Andrew is a simple, foolish fellow, and Sir Toby teases him. He tells him that – with Sir Toby's help – he can win Olivia's hand in marriage. He encourages Sir Andrew to show off his talents as a dancer.

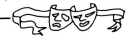

> **Sir Toby urging Sir Andrew to dance**
> *No, Sir, it is legs and thighs. Let*
> *me see thee caper. Ha, higher!*
> *Ha, ha, excellent!*
>
> Act I Sc iii

Viola becomes the page Cesario

After only a few days in the Duke's court, Viola has won Orsino's confidence, and she has fallen in love with him. He knows her as the pageboy called Cesario and sends her to bear messages of his love to Olivia. She agrees to do so but with reluctance because of her own love for the Duke.

Olivia with her household

Among Olivia's servants is the Clown, Feste. Because she is in mourning, Olivia has little patience for Feste's efforts to amuse her. The steward of her household is Malvolio. He is serious and self-important. He dislikes frivolity of any kind, so he disapproves of the Clown – and even more of Sir Toby and Sir Andrew.

When Maria announces that there is a young man at the gate, Malvolio is sent to deal with him. But Malvolio returns to say that the youth insists on seeing Olivia. According to Malvolio, he is 'well favoured' and this arouses Olivia's curiosity. Putting on her mourning veil, she agrees to see him.

Viola disguised as Cesario has prepared her speech and asks Olivia to draw her veil so that she can see her face. When she does, Viola is struck by Olivia's beauty and declares she should not keep it hidden from the world. Olivia replies with a joke, saying she will leave a copy of it in her will.

> **Olivia on her beauty**
> *. . I will give out divers schedules of my beauty. It shall be*
> *inventoried, and every particle and utensil labelled to my will. As,*
> *item, two lips indifferent red; item, two grey eyes, with lids to them;*
> *item, one neck, one chin, and so forth.*
>
> Act I Sc v

Olivia says that she cannot return Orsino's love. Then Viola declares what *she* would do if she were as deeply in love as Orsino is with Olivia.

> **How Viola would woo a lover**
> *Make me a willow cabin at your gate,*
> *And call upon my soul within the house;*
> *Write loyal cantons of contemned love,*
> *And sing them loud even in the dead of night;*
> *Halloo your name to the reverberate hills,*
> *And make the babbling gossip of the air*
> *Cry out 'Olivia!' O, you should not rest*
> *Between the elements of air and earth,*
> *But you should pity me.*
>
> Act I Sc v

Olivia is touched by this speech but again says she cannot love Orsino. She urges Cesario to return to see her, and when he leaves, she realises she has fallen in love with the page. Pretending that he has left a ring behind, she sends Malvolio after him, asking him to return the following day.

Sebastian is alive

By good luck Viola's twin brother, Sebastian, has survived the shipwreck. He was rescued by Antonio, a sea captain. Sebastian thinks Viola is probably dead but he wants to go to Orsino's court. Antonio, who is in trouble with the authorities in Illyria, reluctantly agrees to go with him. Meanwhile, Malvolio has delivered the ring to Viola. She realises that Olivia has fallen in love with 'Cesario'. Somehow she must solve this problem; everything has become too complicated. Viola has fallen in love with Orsino but he is in love with Olivia. Olivia is in love with Cesario – who is Viola disguised as a boy!

A night of merrymaking

Back in Olivia's house, Sir Toby, Sir Andrew and the Clown are enjoying a jolly evening drinking and talking. Just after the Clown has entertained the company with a love song, Maria arrives. It is well after midnight and she complains about the noise. Olivia has been disturbed and has sent Malvolio to put a stop to the celebrations.

Malvolio appears at the door, speaking sternly to the revellers. He warns that, if they do not stop their noisy merrymaking, they will be thrown out of the house.

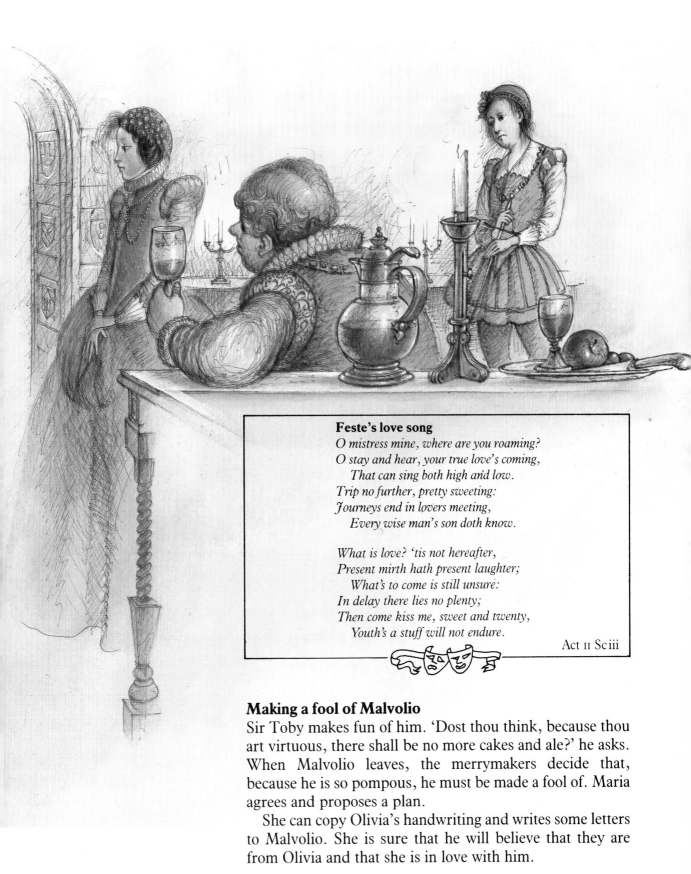

Feste's love song

O mistress mine, where are you roaming?
O stay and hear, your true love's coming,
*   That can sing both high and low.*
Trip no further, pretty sweeting:
Journeys end in lovers meeting,
*   Every wise man's son doth know.*

What is love? 'tis not hereafter,
Present mirth hath present laughter;
*   What's to come is still unsure:*
In delay there lies no plenty;
Then come kiss me, sweet and twenty,
*   Youth's a stuff will not endure.*

Act II Sc iii

Making a fool of Malvolio

Sir Toby makes fun of him. 'Dost thou think, because thou art virtuous, there shall be no more cakes and ale?' he asks. When Malvolio leaves, the merrymakers decide that, because he is so pompous, he must be made a fool of. Maria agrees and proposes a plan.

She can copy Olivia's handwriting and writes some letters to Malvolio. She is sure that he will believe that they are from Olivia and that she is in love with him.

Duke Orsino is lovesick

Back in his palace, the Duke is sad and thoughtful. As usual, he calls for music to ease his feelings.

> ### Orsino calls for music
> *Give me some music. Now good morrow, friends.*
> *Now, good Cesario, but that piece of song,*
> *That old and antique song we heard last night;*
> *Methought it did relieve my passion much,*
> *More than light airs and recollected terms*
> *Of these most brisk and giddy-paced times . . .*
>
> *Mark it, Cesario, it is old and plain;*
> *The spinsters and the knitters in the sun,*
> *And the free maids that weave their thread with bones*
> *Do use to chant it; it is silly sooth,*
> *And dallies with the innocence of love,*
> *Like the old age.*
>
> Act II Sc iv

As the court musicians play, Orsino talks to his page about love, saying how much suffering it causes.

> ### Orsino on the sufferings of love
> *Come hither, boy. If ever thou shalt love,*
> *In the sweet pangs of it remember me:*
> *For such as I am, all true lovers are,*
> *Unstaid and skittish in all motions else,*
> *Save in the constant image of the creature*
> *That is belov'd.*
>
> Act II Sc iv

Orsino is surprised when Viola talks herself with such feeling about love. But he advises that a youth should not marry an older woman.

> ### Orsino's advice
> *. . . Let still the woman take*
> *An elder than herself, so wears she to him,*
> *So sways she level in her husband's heart:*
> *For, boy, however we do praise ourselves,*
> *Our fancies are more giddy and unfirm,*
> *More longing, wavering, sooner lost and worn,*
> *Than women's are.*
>
> Act II Sc iv

Viola tells him of a woman's constancy in love; she is, of course, expressing her own feelings although the Duke does not know this.

Viola on a woman's love

. . . She never told her love,
But let concealment, like a worm i' the bud,
Feed on her damask cheek: she pin'd in thought;
And with a green and yellow melancholy
She sat like Patience on a monument,
Smiling at grief. Was not this love indeed?
We men may say more, swear more, but indeed
Our shows are more than will: for still we prove
Much in our vows, but little in our love.

Act II Sc iv

How Malvolio is tricked

Maria has hidden the letters in a spot where she knows Malvolio will find them. Then she – with Sir Toby and Sir Andrew – hide in a box tree to watch what happens. Just as planned, Malvolio finds the letters and proudly believes that they are a secret confession of Olivia's love for him. Following the instructions in the letters, he goes off to don yellow stockings with cross garters.

> **What Malvolio reads**
> *Some are born great, some achieve greatness, and some have greatness thrust upon them.*
>
> Act II Sc v

Viola now goes off to see Olivia, as she promised the Duke she would. But this meeting becomes very awkward when Olivia confesses her love for Cesario. Viola departs as quickly as she can.

A duel is planned

In order to egg Sir Andrew on in his wooing of Olivia, Sir Toby and Fabian, another member of Olivia's household, suggest that he challenge Cesario to a duel. Just at that moment, Maria announces that Malvolio has been seen – in yellow stockings, cross-gartered and with a silly smile.

Malvolio's 'very strange manner'

When Olivia sees Malvolio, she is surprised at his appearance – and even more so when he calls her 'sweetheart'. She thinks he is suffering from midsummer madness and tells Maria and Sir Toby to take care of him. They, however, tease him more and lock him away.

Meanwhile Sir Andrew has written a letter challenging Viola to a duel. Sir Toby tells Viola and Sir Andrew, separately, how skilful their opponent is with a sword. In fact, neither is at all brave or skilful!

Sebastian and Antonio in Illyria

While all this has been going on, Sebastian has made his way to the main town in Illyria. His friend, Antonio, has followed in secret because he is wanted by the police. He gives Sebastian some money to explore the city, arranging to meet him later at an inn.

60

How the duel is stopped

Both Sir Andrew and Viola are terrified of fighting the duel, but urged on by Sir Toby and Fabian they draw swords. Just then, Antonio appears and leaps to Viola's defence. But, alas, the officers of the law have spotted him and he is immediately arrested. Because they are identical twins, Antonio thinks Viola is Sebastian, so he is surprised and angry when Viola cannot give him money.

Love at first sight

Meanwhile, a confused Sebastian has been taken by the Clown to see Olivia. The moment he meets Olivia, he falls in love with her. As if in a dream, he readily agrees to become betrothed to her. She, of course, thinks he is Cesario.

Sir Topas, the curate, visits Malvolio

Poor Malvolio continues to be tormented by the Clown, who has dressed up as the curate, Sir Topas. He tries to convince Malvolio that he is mad, then leaves him locked up.

A formal betrothal takes place

Sebastian is concerned because he has not found Antonio at the inn, but he is overjoyed that Olivia seems to be in love with him. Puzzled though he is, he goes with her to her chapel to swear a formal betrothal before the priest.

Olivia leads Sebastian to the priest
Blame not this haste of mine. If you mean well,
Now go with me, and with this holy man,
Into the chantry by: there before him,
And underneath that consecrated roof,
Plight me the full assurance of your faith,
That my most jealous and too doubtful soul
May live at peace.

Act IV Sc iii

Mistaken identity

Orsino, with Viola, arrives at Olivia's house to court her in person but just then, Antonio and the law officers appear. Viola points out to the Duke that Antonio was the man who rescued her in the duel. But the sea captain turns on her, calling her ungrateful.

When Olivia appears, there is even more confusion. She tells the Duke that she must reject his love because 'Cesario'

is her betrothed. Viola, alarmed, declares she must follow Orsino.

> **Viola follows the Duke**
> . . . *After him I love*
> *More than I love these eyes, more than my life,*
> *More, by all mores, than e'er I shall love wife.* Act v Sc i

The priest arrives and confirms Olivia's story. With this, the Duke orders Viola out of his sight; she has betrayed him.

Just at that moment Sir Toby and Sir Andrew appear, followed by Sebastian. Everyone sees at once how similar the two young people are. Sebastian speaks lovingly to Olivia and greets Antonio with affection. Viola is overjoyed to see Sebastian, the twin brother she feared dead. She reveals that she is disguised.

A double wedding is planned
When Orsino realises that the page he has grown so fond of is a girl, he at once decides to marry her. Olivia, pleased that the mix-up is sorted out, suggests a double wedding.

Olivia orders that Malvolio be released and brought before her. She recognises Maria's handwriting on the letters and explains to Malvolio how he has been tricked.

His pride and vanity have been deeply hurt and he vows revenge – on Maria and Sir Toby (who, it seems, have also just married). He storms out leaving the Clown to sing the last words of the play.

The Clown's song
When that I was and a little tiny boy,
With hey, ho, the wind and the rain,
A foolish thing was but a toy,
For the rain it raineth every day.

But when I came to man's estate,
With hey, ho, the wind and the rain,
'Gainst knaves and thieves men shut their gates,
For the rain it raineth every day.

Act v Sci

Characters in Twelfth Night

Viola

Viola is one of Shakespeare's most charming heroines. She is not only beautiful and accomplished, she is also practical and courageous. When she believes her brother is dead, she does not bemoan her fate or go into mourning like Olivia. Instead, she goes out to seek employment. She falls in love with the Duke, but loyally tries to win Olivia for him, keeping her own real love secret. When she tells Orsino how constant and enduring a woman's love can be, we know she means it.

Orsino

A noble duke, in nature as in name

The Duke is young but rather moody. He is in love with the idea of love. His love for Olivia is unlike the real affection he feels for Viola. He is a cultured man and loves music. Everyone, including Olivia, has a good opinion of him. When he proposes to Viola, we feel sure they will make a happy couple.

Olivia

Olivia is a beautiful countess. Although young, she is a capable and determined woman. At first she grieves too much for her brother, but when she falls in love with Cesario, she is keen to marry him quickly. She is generous not only to Sir Toby but also to Malvolio, and she runs her household well. She firmly refuses Orsino's love but adapts herself, when she falls in love, to changed circumstances.

Orsino

Viola

Malvolio

Malvolio is one of Shakespeare's most famous characters, whom everyone laughs at because he is so pompous and vain. Yet he is a loyal servant to Olivia who is anxious not to lose him.

Although Shakespeare makes fun of him, he is dignified and full of courage when defending himself against the Clown. He has been unfairly tricked and, like Olivia, we feel that he has been 'most notoriously abused.'

Olivia criticises Malvolio
O, you are sick of self-love, Malvolio, and taste with a distempered appetite. To be generous, guiltless, and of free disposition, to take those things for bird-bolts that you deem cannon-bullets.

Act I Sc v

Sir Andrew Aguecheek

I knew 'twas I for many call me fool

Sir Andrew is a true comic character. He is silly, cowardly and never suspects that he is being used and tricked by Sir Toby. He enjoys merrymaking with Sir Toby and has no great ambition in life. When Sir Toby asks him, 'Does not life consist of the four elements?' he replies, 'I think rather it consists of eating and drinking.'

Sir Toby Belch

I am sure care's an enemy of life.

Sir Toby is intent on enjoying himself, usually at other people's expense. Even though he is a bully, a cheat and a drunkard, he is a likeable rogue who is always cheerful. When he marries the quick-witted and practical Maria, they are a well-matched pair.

Sir Andrew Aguecheek

Sir Toby Belch

Olivia

Malvolio

Feste, the Clown

Feste, the Clown

In Tudor times, many princes and noblemen employed a jester or clown. Generally, they were witty, amusing and able to sing and dance, just as Feste does. Often they wore brightly coloured costumes, and a cap with bells attached to it. Feste is not a 'natural' fool as Sir Andrew is, but a clever man who can out-talk everyone and win arguments. He enjoys the company of Maria, Sir Toby and Sir Andrew, and sings cheerful songs for them. When with the Duke, he matches his mood by singing melancholy songs.

ROMEO AND JULIET

Illustrations by George Thompson

The story of Romeo and Juliet

In Verona in Italy, a long-standing feud exists between two families – the Montagues and the Capulets. When their servants meet in the street, they quarrel, and this is how the play opens – with a street brawl.

A street battle
Benvolio who is a Montague tries to stop the fight. But Tybalt, who is a Capulet, will not listen. The quarrel turns into a violent battle. This alarms the citizens of Verona – and their ruler, Prince Escalius. The Prince stops the battle. But he declares that any more fighting between the families will be punished by death.

The love-sick Romeo
Benvolio's cousin, Romeo, is unhappy. And his parents are worried about him. Benvolio finds out that Romeo is in love. But the lady does not return his love. Benvolio tells him to look for another lady. But Romeo, of course, says he can never love anyone else.

> **Romeo on the nature of love**
> *Love is a smoke rais'd with the fume of sighs;*
> *Being purg'd, a fire sparkling in lovers' eyes;*
> *Being vex'd, a sea raging with lovers' tears;*
> *What is it else? a madness most discreet,*
> *A choking gall and a preserving sweet.*
>
> Act I Sc i

A proposal of marriage
Juliet's father is Lord Capulet. He has been asked for Juliet's hand in marriage by Count Paris. Although she is very young, Lord Capulet agrees to the marriage – but only if Juliet decides she wants to marry the handsome young Count. He invites Paris to a ball he is giving that night, and sends his servant off to invite other guests. Unfortunately, the servant has never learned to read. So when he meets Romeo and Benvolio in the street, he asks them to read out the list for him.

Why Romeo goes to the ball
One of the guests is Rosaline, the lady with whom Romeo is hopelessly in love. Romeo agrees to gatecrash the ball with Benvolio – but only to catch a glimpse of Rosaline.

Juliet hears of the marriage proposal

Lady Capulet tells Juliet and her Nurse about Paris's marriage proposal. She tells Juliet to look for him at the ball. And to notice how handsome he is. Juliet replies that, if she likes him, she will consider marrying him.

Romeo and his friends go to the ball

Romeo and his friends, Benvolio and Mercutio, wear masks to the ball. (This was common in Shakespeare's time.) Romeo is worried that he will be recognized as a Montague. And he is also troubled by a strange fear, because of a dream he has had. But Mercutio jokes about the dream. He says it was caused by the fairy Queen Mab.

At the Capulets' house, the music and dancing has already begun. Romeo, who decides not to dance, notices Juliet. He immediately thinks how beautiful she is. But just then Romeo is recognized by Tybalt. He is furious that a Montague is at the ball. He wants to kill Romeo. But he is stopped from doing anything by Juliet's father who sternly tells Tybalt to behave himself.

Romeo meets Juliet

When the dance ends, Romeo goes up to Juliet. He touches her hand and they begin to talk. They fall instantly in love with each other, and kiss – just before they are parted by the

Nurse. She tells Romeo that Juliet is the daughter of the house. Horrified, Romeo realizes that he has fallen in love with a Capulet. And he hurries away from the ball with Benvolio. As the guests leave, Juliet asks the Nurse about Romeo. She learns that he is the Montagues' only son. She, too, is struck with horror.

Lady Capulet describes Paris
This precious book of love, this unbound lover,
To beautify him, only lacks a cover:　　　　Act I Sc iii

Queen Mab's carriage
Her chariot is an empty hazelnut,
Made by the joiner squirrel or old grub,
Time out o' mind the fairies' coachmakers.
And in this state she gallops night by night
Through lovers' brains, and then they dream of love;
　　　　Act I Sc iv

Juliet on the balcony

After the ball is over, Romeo escapes from his friends. Jumping over the wall into the Capulets' orchard, he sees Juliet on a balcony. He is dazzled by her beauty. She does not know that Romeo can see and hear her. And she declares her love for him – even though his name is Montague.

Romeo on seeing Juliet on the balcony
But soft! what light through yonder window breaks?
It is the east, and Juliet is the sun!
. . . her eyes in heaven
Would through the airy region stream so bright
That birds would sing and think it were not night.　　Act II Sc ii

Juliet on Romeo's name
O Romeo, Romeo! wherefore art thou Romeo?
. . . O, be some other name!
What's in a name? that which we call a rose
By any other name would smell as sweet;
　　　　Act II Sc ii

Romeo and Juliet declare their love

Romeo calls to Juliet. And she recognizes his voice. He swears his love for her – and she for him – in the most beautiful words. They agree to marry the next day. But they can hardly bear to part.

Romeo swears his love

Lady, by yonder blessed moon I swear,
That tips with silver all these fruit-tree tops, –

Juliet declares her love

My bounty is as boundless as the sea,
My love as deep; the more I give to thee,
The more I have, for both are infinite.

Juliet's parting words

Good-night, good-night! parting is such sweet sorrow
That I shall say good-night till it be morrow.

Act II Sc ii

71

Romeo arranges the marriage

As dawn breaks, Romeo goes to see his father confessor, Friar Laurence. The priest is surprised that Romeo is now in love with Juliet. But he agrees to marry the lovers. He hopes it might reconcile their families.

Meanwhile Mercutio and Benvolio have been looking for Romeo. They know he did not come home the night before. Tybalt has sent a letter challenging him to a duel. When Romeo appears, he is in a cheerful mood. He jokes with his friends. Then he asks Juliet's Nurse to tell her about the wedding. It is to be that afternoon.

The marriage ceremony

Juliet has been waiting anxiously for the Nurse to return. The Nurse is a silly woman. She chatters on before telling Juliet the time of the wedding. Juliet is delighted, and she rushes off to meet Romeo and the Friar.

Friar Laurence is ready to perform the marriage ceremony. But he is uneasy. He warns Romeo about hasty marriages. It seems as if he is prophesying the lovers' tragic deaths. But the wedding takes place. And Romeo and Juliet arrange to see each other that night.

> **The Friar's warning**
> *These violent delights have violent ends,*
> *And in their triumph die . . .*
> *Therefore, love moderately; long love doth so;*
>
> Act II Sc vi

A fatal duel takes place

Mercutio and Benvolio are walking in the street when they meet Tybalt. He is looking for Romeo. He is still angry that Romeo went to the Capulet ball. Just then, Romeo arrives. Tybalt insults him and calls him a villain. But Romeo does not want to fight. Juliet's family are like his own now he is married. But Mercutio is furious. He thinks Romeo is a coward. He draws his sword and attacks Tybalt. Romeo urges them to stop. But as he tries to break them apart, Tybalt stabs Mercutio to death.

Romeo gets his revenge

Romeo is grief stricken at Mercutio's death. He died defending Romeo. Romeo seeks out Tybalt, and they fight a duel. Tybalt is killed. Prince Escalius hears of the murders. He banishes Romeo from Verona instead of

ordering his execution. But this is small comfort for Romeo.

Juliet learns of Romeo's banishment
Meanwhile, Juliet is longing for night to come, when Romeo is to visit her.

Juliet longs for nightfall

Come, gentle night, come, loving, black-brow'd night,
Give me my Romeo; and, when he shall die,
Take him and cut him out in little stars,
And he will make the face of heaven so fine,
That all the world will be in love with night,

Act III Sc ii

Just then, her Nurse rushes in with the news of Tybalt's death and Romeo's banishment. Juliet is full of sorrow. Her meeting with Romeo will be a last farewell.

Since the fight, Romeo has been hiding with Friar Laurence. When the Nurse brings him news of Juliet's unhappiness, he is very upset, and wants to kill himself. But the Friar urges him to see Juliet – and then to leave for Mantua.

Lord Capulet arranges a marriage
Paris still wishes to marry Juliet. Now suddenly Lord Capulet agrees to the wedding – but without asking Juliet about her feelings. He arranges for it to take place in three days' time.

Romeo and Juliet's farewell

Romeo has secretly spent the night with Juliet. As dawn breaks, he knows he must hurry away – or else be captured.

At the break of day

Jul. Wilt thou be gone? it is not yet near day;
It was the nightingale, and not the lark,
That pierc'd the fearful hollow of thine ear;
Nightly she sings on yon pomegranate-tree:
Believe me, love, it was the nightingale.

Rom. It was the lark, the herald of the morn,
No nightingale: look, love, what envious streaks
Do lace the severing clouds in yonder east:
Night's candles are burnt out, and jocund day
Stands tiptoe on the misty mountain tops:

Romeo's and Juliet's farewell

Rom. Farewell, farewell! one kiss, and I'll descend.
Jul. Art thou gone so? my lord, my love, my friend!
I must hear from thee every day in the hour,
For in a minute there are many days:
O! by this count I shall be much in years
Ere I again behold my Romeo.

Act III Sc v

The lovers find it difficult to part. But as Romeo climbs down the balcony, they bid each other farewell.

Juliet refuses to marry Paris

Just as Romeo leaves, Juliet learns from her mother that she is to marry Paris in three days' time. Juliet is angry and refuses to marry the Count. When her father hears this, he is furious. He tells Juliet she is proud and ungrateful. He orders her to marry Paris – or else be dragged to the church.

> **Lord Capulet's threat**
> *Look to 't, think on 't, I do not use to jest.*
> *Thursday is near; lay hand on heart, advise:*
> *An you be mine, I'll give you to my friend;*
> *An you be not, hang, beg, starve, die in the streets.*
> *For, by my soul, I'll ne'er acknowledge thee,*
> *Nor what is mine shall never do thee good:*
>
> Act III Sc v

Juliet appeals to her mother. She asks her to delay the marriage. But her mother refuses to listen. In desperation, Juliet asks the Nurse's advice. The woman cheerfully says Juliet should marry Paris. She points out that Romeo is not likely to return. Juliet realizes that everyone is against her. She decides to ask Friar Laurence to help.

The Friar's plan to stop the marriage

Juliet tells the Friar that she cannot marry Paris. She would rather kill herself, she says. Seeing her so desperate, the priest makes a plan. He knows of a sleeping potion which can make a person appear dead. But after some time, the person who takes it wakes up – just as if they had been asleep. The Friar tells Juliet to agree to marry Paris. After she has taken the potion, her family will think she is dead.

She will be placed in a tomb. But when she wakes, Romeo will be with her. Then they can both flee to Mantua. Friar Laurence says he will tell Romeo the plan by letter – so that Romeo can come back to Verona in secret. Juliet agrees to the plan and goes home.

The wedding preparations

Juliet tells her father that she will marry Paris. Lord Capulet is delighted, so much so that he brings the wedding forward by a day! Will this upset the Friar's plan? In great excitement Capulet goes off to make the preparations for the wedding. Juliet and her Nurse decide on the wedding clothes. Then Juliet sends both her Nurse and her mother away. She tells them she wants to pray before the marriage ceremony. But really, she is plucking up her courage to take the sleeping potion.

Juliet is frightened

Juliet knows she must now swallow the sleeping potion. But she is very frightened. 'I have a faint cold fear thrills through my veins, That almost freezes up the heat of life,' she says. She worries that the potion may not work. Will she wake up before Romeo arrives? Will she see Tybalt's dead body? Will spirits haunt the tomb? But for Romeo's sake she *must* take the potion. She lies on her bed. Then she swallows the mixture. She falls back as the bottle drops from her hand.

How Juliet is found dead

The time has come to dress for the wedding ceremony. The Nurse goes to wake Juliet. She draws the curtain. But Juliet does not wake up when she calls. She now realizes that the girl is dead. She screams for help. And then the Capulets rush in – followed by the Friar and Paris. Juliet's parents pour out their grief. They are interrupted by the Friar. He knows, of course, that Juliet is not really dead. He says they must arrange for the burial and carry Juliet's body to the church.

Capulet on Juliet's death
Her blood is settled, and her joints are stiff;
Life and these lips have long been separated.
Death lies on her like an untimely frost
Upon the sweetest flower of all the field.

Act IV Sc v

What happens to Romeo in Mantua

In Mantua, Romeo has a dream that Juliet finds him dead. In fact, he learns from his servant that Juliet is dead. He decides to go at once to Verona. He buys some poison. When he arrives, he intends to kill himself in the vault where Juliet lies.

How the Friar's plan goes awry

Back in Verona, the Friar learns that his letter to Romeo was never delivered. His messenger was prevented by plague from leaving Verona. Juliet is to wake up in three hours – so Friar Laurence hurries off to the tomb.

The Friar's advice to the Capulets

She's not well married that lives married long,
But she's best married that dies married young.
Dry up your tears, and stick your rosemary
On this fair corse and, as the custom is,
In all her best array bear her to church:　　　Act IV Sc v

Romeo's dream in Mantua

I dreamt my lady came and found me dead –
Strange dream, that gives a dead man leave to think!
And breath'd such life with kisses in my lips,
That I reviv'd and was an emperor.

Act V Sc i

Romeo and Paris meet at Juliet's tomb

Paris is mourning at Juliet's tomb when he spies Romeo.

He thinks he is there for evil purposes. He challenges Romeo, and they fight a duel. Only after he falls, does Romeo realize he has killed Paris.

The death of Romeo

Romeo opens Juliet's tomb. He gazes lovingly on his bride.

Romeo gazes on Juliet

. . . Ah, dear Juliet,
Why art thou yet so fair? Shall I believe
That unsubstantial death is amorous,
And that the lean abhorred monster keeps
Thee here in dark to be his paramour?

Act v Sc iii

Romeo then prepares himself to die.

Romeo's last kiss

. . . Eyes, look your last!
Arms, take your last embrace! and, lips, O you
The doors of breath, seal with a righteous kiss . . .

Act v Sc iii

He drinks the poison and dies.

Juliet awakes

Just as Juliet wakes up, the Friar arrives. He sees the bodies of Paris and Romeo. He tells Juliet they must fly away at once. When Juliet realizes that Romeo is dead, she refuses to leave. She sees that he has taken poison. 'O churl! drink all, and leave no friendly drop To help me after?' she says. She kisses his lips. Then she takes up Romeo's dagger to stab herself. Just as she does, she hears noise outside. Paris's servant has summoned help.

The bodies are discovered

The servant has summoned the help of a watchman. They enter the tomb and find the bodies of Romeo, Paris and Juliet. They send a messenger to bring the Prince and the Capulets and Montagues to the tomb. The Friar has been arrested in the churchyard. He is trembling and sorrowful. And he is suspected of the murders.

Just then, the Prince arrives. He is followed by the Capulets. They are horrified to see Juliet stabbed and bleeding. When Lord Montague appears, he too is shocked and grief-stricken.

The Friar explains the tragedy

The Prince demands to know what has happened. The Friar begins to explain how the events took place. He partly blames himself for the lovers' deaths. He tells how he married Romeo and Juliet. Then he describes how the lovers were affected by Tybalt's death and Romeo's banishment. He explains the plan he hatched. And how his letter failed to reach Romeo in Mantua. Then he offers to die himself – for taking part in the tragedy.

The story is confirmed by Romeo's servant

Romeo's servant explains how he broke the news of Juliet's death and how he and Romeo set off at once for Verona. Still in his hand he carried a letter from Romeo to his father.

Romeo's letter confirms all that has been said. And the Prince decides that nobody will be punished for the deaths. Everybody, he says, has suffered enough. But he does put the blame for the tragedy on the Capulet and Montague feud.

> **The Prince blames the Capulets and Montagues**
> *. . . Capulet! Montague!*
> *See, what a scourge is laid upon your hate,*
> *That heaven finds means to kill your joys with love,*
> *And I, for winking at your discords too,*
> *Have lost a brace of kinsmen: all are punish'd.*
>
> Act v Sc iii

The Montagues and Capulets are reconciled

The Montagues and Capulets now agree that their feud is over. And they declare they will build statues to honour the lovers. The Prince speaks the last words of tribute to the lovers.

> **The Prince on the story of Romeo and Juliet.**
> *Go hence, to have more talk of these sad things;*
> *Some shall be pardon'd and some punished:*
> *For never was a story of more woe*
> *Than this of Juliet and her Romeo.*
>
> Act v Sc iii

Characters in Romeo and Juliet

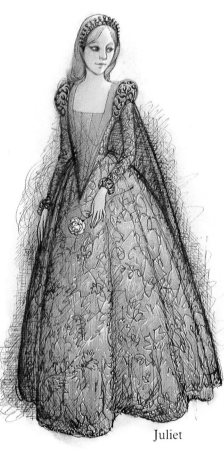

Juliet

Juliet
Juliet is a young girl, only 14 years of age. She is a gentle person and obedient to her parents. And she is fond of the Nurse who has looked after her since she was a baby. She belongs to a noble family from Verona. Her cousin is the quick-tempered young man, Tybalt. Probably because she is so young, Juliet does not have friends outside her family. This is a shame – because when her family force her to marry Paris she has no young person to turn to for advice.

In a way, falling in love makes Juliet more grown-up. Now she does not rely on her parents, but makes up her own mind. Her first thoughts are for Romeo. After Romeo is banished, she does not beg him to stay. This is because she knows he will be captured. Her love for Romeo becomes the most important thing in life. In the end, she prefers to die rather than live her life without him.

Romeo
Romeo is a person who rushes into things without thinking. When he hears that Juliet is dead, he sets off straight away for Verona. And we know he has bought poison to kill himself. But he is a kind-hearted, good man. He did not want to kill Tybalt. He is generous and kind to his friends and his servant. And when he kills Paris, he feels very sad.

Falling in love with Juliet helps Romeo to grow up. At the beginning of the play, he feels sorry for himself. But at the end, he thinks of Juliet and not himself. When he kills himself it is to be reunited with her.

Romeo

Lord and Lady Capulet
Lord Capulet is a stubborn old man. And he can also be short-tempered. He loves his only daughter and wants the best for her.

Lady Capulet is much younger than her husband. She is an aristocratic lady, and not very warm-hearted. Although she probably loves Juliet, she is not as close to her as the Nurse is. She thinks it is best for Juliet to marry a suitable person like Paris, even if she does not love him. She hates Romeo and plans to poison him after he has killed Tybalt. She keeps the feud going more than her husband.

Lord and Lady Capulet

Mercutio

Mercutio is one of the most likeable characters in the play. He is young and lively. And he is always talking and joking. He teases Romeo about being in love with Rosaline.

He is also loyal and honourable. When Romeo is insulted by Tybalt, he springs to his defence. Even as he dies from the wounds inflicted by Tybalt's sword, he is brave. He pretends that it is only 'a scratch'. His death is one of the saddest parts of the play.

Tybalt

Tybalt is a quarrelsome young man. He is a troublemaker who loves fighting. He is very angry when Romeo appears at the Capulets' ball. He wants to fight him straight away. He is only prevented from doing this by Juliet's father. More than anyone else, he is the person who keeps the feud between the Montagues and the Capulets alive. He likes violence for its own sake. When he is killed by Romeo, we are not particularly sorry.

The Nurse

Juliet's Nurse is a down-to-earth, rather stupid woman. She nursed Juliet as a baby and still fusses over her. She loves her like her own child. Juliet is very fond of the Nurse. She confides in her – telling her about Romeo and the wedding. But when Romeo is banished, the Nurse advises Juliet to marry Paris. This is the sensible thing to do, she tells Juliet. Juliet is shocked. She realizes that the Nurse does not understand how deep her love for Romeo is. Sadly, she is unable to talk to her any more about her feelings.

Paris

Paris is a handsome young man, pleasant and courteous. Because he is a cousin of the Prince of Verona, he is a most eligible suitor for Juliet. He courts her in the correct way – by asking permission from her father. Paris seems to care truly for Juliet. He sorrowfully mourns at her grave. He is also brave when he approaches Romeo at the tomb and dies in the fight. Romeo is saddened at his death. He knows that Paris was an honourable man.

Mercutio

Tybalt

Friar Laurence

Friar Laurence is a wise and holy man. He is a priest and the person to whom both Romeo and Juliet turn to for advice. And usually, he gives them good advice. Some people say, though, that he should not have married the lovers in secret. They say that it was wrong to deceive the parents of Romeo and Juliet. For a moment, even Juliet thinks the Friar regrets his part in the marriage. She thinks the sleeping potion he gave her may be a poison.

The Friar tells of his part in the tragic events. Perhaps he could have prevented them, he says. He is willing to be punished by the Prince if he is found guilty. But the Prince admires his honesty – and pardons him. Like the Montagues and Capulets, Friar Laurence has suffered enough for his part in the tragedy.

Friar Laurence   The Nurse   Paris

JULIUS CAESAR

Illustrations by Roger Payne

The story of Julius Caesar

The Roman streets are filled with rejoicing citizens. It is the feast of Lupercal, which celebrates the founding of Rome. The people have another cause for celebration; Julius Caesar has returned from the battlefield, having defeated his enemy, Pompey the Great. As he walks in procession through the city to the sounds of drums and trumpets, a cheering crowd makes way for him. Suddenly, Caesar hears someone call to him and he pauses to listen. 'Beware the Ides of March,' a soothsayer tells him. Caesar scoffs at this warning and dismisses the fortune teller. 'He is a dreamer; let us leave him; pass.'

Caesar for emperor?

As the procession moves on, two Roman noblemen linger behind. One is Brutus, whose ancestors helped found the republic of Rome; the other is Cassius, who fears that Caesar has become too ambitious. Cassius points out that Caesar secretly wants to be king and emperor of Rome and to destroy the power of the senators who rule the city.

Brutus is reluctant to discuss Caesar with Cassius but when he hears cries from the crowd in praise of Caesar, he admits that Caesar has become too full of himself.

Dangerous Cassius

At this moment, Caesar returns from the procession and it is obvious that he is not happy. He sees Cassius and explains to his young friend, the soldier Mark Antony, why he dislikes the man.

Caesar moves on but Casca, another senator, tells Brutus and Cassius that three times Caesar refused the crown – but only because the people did not want him to accept it. Disappointment was the reason for Caesar's sullen looks.

A conspiracy is born

Cassius has arranged to meet Casca in the evening and, as night falls, thunder and lightning disturb the sky – warnings of evil, says Cassius. Both men agree that Caesar is a threat to Rome and must be killed. There are other men who will join the conspiracy, but they need Brutus's support because he is popular with the people.

Brutus is troubled

In the small hours of the night, Brutus walks alone in his garden, brooding over his talk with Cassius. Brutus does not want to see Rome ruled by a tyrant. Although he loves Caesar as a friend, he really does fear that Caesar may seize power for himself. Arguing with himself, he finally decides – like the conspirators – that Caesar must be killed.

Just as he asks his boy servant, Lucius, to check the date (the day about to dawn is the Ides of March!), there is a knocking at the gate. It is Cassius with a group of men whose faces are hidden by their cloaks.

Portia chides Brutus

...Am I yourself
But, as it were, in sort of limitation,
To keep with you at meals, comfort your bed,
And talk to you sometimes?

Act ii Sc i

Cassius's friends are the other conspirators, all noblemen of Rome who have decided that Caesar must die.

Introducing the conspirators
Cassius introduces the men as Trebonius, Decius, Casca, Cinna and Metellus. Cassius explains that they have planned to kill Caesar that very day in the Capitol. Brutus agrees to the plan but declares that Mark Antony should not be killed. 'Let us be sacrificers, but not butchers,' he says.

Portia's pleas
The conspirators soon leave but Brutus's wife, Portia, who has seen the men, is worried. Her husband has been irritable and anxious and she knows that there is something on his mind. Portia begs Brutus to confide in her about his troubles.

Calphurnia's dream
Caesar's wife, Calphurnia, has had a nightmare. In her dream she saw Caesar's statue pouring with blood and she begs her husband not to go to the Capitol. Caesar tells her that people must not be afraid of death. If it will please her, however, he agrees not to go to the Capitol.

> **A noble Roman woman**
> *A woman well-reputed,*
> *Cato's daughter,*
> *Think you I am no stronger*
> *than my sex,*
> *Being so father'd and so*
> *husbanded?*
>
> Act II Sc i

> **Caesar on death**
> *Cowards die many times before their deaths;*
> *The valiant never taste of death but once.*
> *Of all the wonders that I yet have heard,*
> *It seems to me most strange that men should fear;*
> *Seeing that death, a necessary end,*
> *Will come when it will come.*
>
> Act II Sc ii

Hearing that Caesar is to remain at home, the conspirator Decius tells Caesar that this very day the senators are to offer him the crown. Caesar at once changes his mind and sets off. Both a teacher, Artemidorus (who has discovered the plot), and the soothsayer try to warn Caesar – but fail. Inside the Capitol, he is greeted by the conspirators.

The death of Caesar
According to plan, they surround him, with Brutus kneeling at his feet. Casca lifts his dagger first and together they plunge their weapons into Caesar's body. Although he struggles, Caesar is overcome by his wounds. He sees, sadly,

that his beloved Brutus is among his attackers and, as he falls, he utters a pathetic reproach to his old friend. 'And you too, Brutus?,' he says and then he dies. His body falls at the foot of the statue of Pompey, the great general he conquered. For the conspirators, the killing of Caesar was a solemn sacrifice, and they bathe their hands in his blood.

The murder causes uproar among the senators. Amid the shouts and screams, Brutus tries to restore order. Mark Antony, shocked and angry at the murder, remains cold and

calm. All he asks is permission to speak at Caesar's funeral.

Left alone with Caesar's body, the grief-stricken Antony rages against the murderers, promising death and war in revenge.

Caesar's funeral

A large crowd has gathered to hear Brutus explain why Caesar had to die. Brutus speaks of his great love for Caesar, but of his greater love for Rome. Caesar was ambitious, he tells the people, and would have made slaves of them all.

Mark Antony's lament
O! pardon me, thou bleeding piece of earth,
That I am meek and gentle with these butchers;
Thou art the ruins of the noblest man
That ever lived in the tide of times.
Woe to the hand that shed this costly blood!

Act III Sc i

Because Brutus's words are so eloquent, the citizens believe him.

Then Mark Antony appears, carrying the body of Caesar. He explains that he is simply trying to work out why Caesar had to die; he was a good and generous man who refused the crown. But if Brutus and the others say he was ambitious, then they must be right. Waving Caesar's will, he announces that Caesar has left all his riches to the people. Weeping over Caesar's body, he asks, 'Here was a Caesar! When comes such another?' The people, deeply moved by Antony's words and feelings, shout their support for him.

Antony's funeral oration

Friends, Romans, countrymen, lend me your ears;
I come to bury Caesar, not to praise him.
The evil that men do lives after them,
The good is oft interred with their bones;
So let it be with Caesar. The noble Brutus
Hath told you Caesar was ambitious;
If it were so, it was a grievous fault,
And grievously hath Caesar answer'd it . . .
When that the poor have cried, Caesar hath wept;
Ambition should be made of sterner stuff:
Yet Brutus says he was ambitious;
And Brutus is an honourable man.

Act III Sc ii

Civil war and discord

Antony joins forces with Octavius, Caesar's nephew, who has just returned to Rome, and with a gallant general, Lepidus. But Antony has no confidence in Lepidus and wants to cast him aside so that there will be more power – and money – for himself and Octavius.

Meanwhile, Brutus and Cassius have fled from Rome to raise an army. They too have quarrelled because Cassius and his friends have accepted bribes. Brutus expresses his disapproval in no uncertain terms. Cassius is heartbroken by his scornful remarks and invites Brutus to kill him. 'A friend should bear his friend's infirmities, but Brutus makes mine greater than they are,' he laments. Brutus, touched by Cassius's feelings, confesses his own grief over the suicide of Portia in Rome. Making up their quarrel, they agree on a battle plan – although Brutus rejects a sensible strategy by Cassius in favour of his own ideas. They will meet to fight the enemy at a place called Philippi.

The need for action

There is a tide in the affairs of men,
Which, taken at the flood, leads on to fortune;
Omitted, all the voyage of their life
Is bound in shallows and in miseries

Act IV Sc iii

Enter the ghost of Caesar

Left alone with his sleeping servant, Brutus sees something as his candle flickers. It is the ghost of Caesar who declares that he is 'thy evil spirit, Brutus .... thou shalt see me at Philippi.' The ghost disappears and Brutus, shaking with fear, pulls himself together.

On the plains of Philippi

Antony and Octavius, too, have made plans for the battle to come. The leaders of the opposing armies meet in a last chance to make peace. It is clear that this is not possible. Both sides insult each other and swear revenge. Retiring to their camps, they prepare for the battle.

Brutus and Cassius exchange farewells

Cassius is gloomy because he has seen evil omens and fears that their army may lose the fight. Brutus, too, is in low spirits. The two friends talk of defeat and death, almost as if they have lost the will to fight. They put on a brave face before making an affectionate farewell. It is the last time they will see each other alive, and they both seem to sense it.

Cassius's defeat

During the course of the battle, Cassius's troops are overthrown by Antony. Brutus's army, though, defeats Octavius. Cassius, angry and in despair, is forced to flee to a safe spot overlooking the battlefield. Seeing some troops approaching, he sends his fellow soldier and old friend, Titinius, to see if they are friend or foe.

Being short-sighted himself, Cassius asks his servant, Pindarus, to watch what happens. Cassius feels doomed. He is sure that this particular day, which is his birthday, is the day on which he will die.

The death of Cassius

Pindarus, seeing Titinius surrounded by soldiers, wrongly thinks that he has been captured by the enemy. For Cassius, the loss of his friend is the final blow. He orders Pindarus to hold the sword – the very weapon he used to kill Caesar – and Cassius kills himself.

In fact, the men that Titinius met on the battlefield were Brutus and his troops. Returning to give the good news to Cassius, Titinius finds him dead. He mourns his dear friend with sad words and then, overcome with grief, he takes his own life.

Brutus finds his comrades dead

Brutus, who has come to greet Cassius, finds the bodies of both these noble warriors. 'Friends, I owe more tears To this dead man than you shall ever see me pay. I shall find time, Cassius, I shall find time,' he says.

Brutus bids farewell to Cassius

. . . but this same day
Must end that work the ides of March begun;
And whether we shall meet again I know not.
Therefore our everlasting farewell take:
For ever and for ever, farewell, Cassius!
If we do meet again, why, we shall smile
If not, why then, this parting was well made.

Act v Sc i

Cassius despairs

This day I breathed first; time is
*   come around,*
And where I did begin, there
*   shall I end;*
My life is run his compass.

Act v Sc iii

In the second stage of the battle, Brutus and his soldiers fight bravely but to no avail. Left with only a small band of followers, Brutus begs each one of them to kill him but they all refuse. He urges them to flee and bids them farewell.

Brutus's farewell to his followers

. . . Countrymen,
My heart doth joy that yet, in all my life,
I found no man but he was true to me.
I shall have glory by this losing day,
More than Octavius and Mark Antony
By this vile conquest shall attain unto.

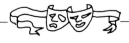

Act v Sc v

Only his servant, Strato, remains and, on Brutus's orders, he holds the sword on which Brutus kills himself.

Enter the victors

Finding Brutus dead, Octavius and Antony pardon all his followers. Antony pays tribute to the man who loved Caesar more than anyone and who killed him not for personal gain but for the good of the state. He was the perfect man.

Antony's tribute to Brutus
This was the noblest Roman of them all;
All the conspirators save only he
Did that they did in envy of great Caesar;
He only, in a general honest thought
And common good to all, made one of them.
His life was gentle, and the elements
So mix'd in him that Nature might stand up
And say to all the world, 'This was a man!'

Act v Sc v

Characters in Julius Caesar

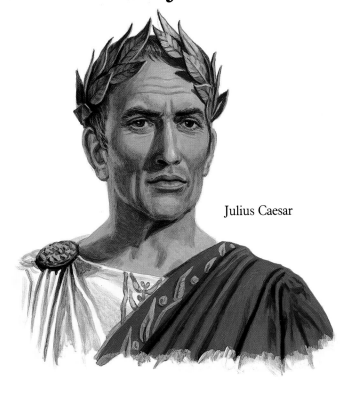

Julius Caesar

The great Caesar
But I am constant as the northern star,
Of whose true-fix'd and resting quality
There is no fellow in the firmament.

Act III Sc i

Brutus

If there is a hero in this tragic play, it is Brutus. 'This was the noblest Roman of them all,' says Mark Antony. He points out that among the conspirators Brutus was the only man whose motives for killing Caesar were pure. Brutus believed that what he was doing was right. It was for the good of the state and to protect the liberty of the Roman people. A gentle, generous and thoughtful man, he has no ambition for himself. Everything he does is for unselfish reasons – for honour.

In a way, Brutus's honesty and high-mindedness are his undoing. He wrongly believes that the conspirators are honourable men, like him. He trusts people too much. He believes what they say, rather than thinking what their motives might be. He is an idealist who does not realise that other men act from evil or selfish motives.

His self-righteousness can be annoying and it angers Cassius on several occasions. 'Brutus,

Julius Caesar

Shakespeare's Julius Caesar is rather different from the real Caesar of Roman history who most people think was the greatest ruler of ancient times. In the play, he is a proud man who acts as if he were already king of Rome. Cassius suggests that he is a coward and that he has fits. He seems to be a foolish and vain man who is not at all noble and great. Only after his death do we realise what a hero he was. Even though Shakespeare casts him in a bad light – to make a contrast with Brutus – he still gives him some of the best lines in the play.

Brutus's idea of honour
If it be aught toward the general good,
Set honour in one eye and death i' the other,
And I will look on both indifferently;
For let the gods so speed me as I love
The name of honour more than I fear death.

Act I Sc ii

Brutus

this sober form of yours hides wrongs,' he says. But Brutus cannot admit this; he is always right. In the end, he dies for his ideals. We admire him for being a great man, but understand how unwise he was to be so inflexible. He is wrong but he dies unrepentant.

Mark Antony

Brutus dismisses Antony as a limb of Caesar, who can do no harm. He thinks he is a frivolous young man who simply likes sports and having a good time. However, when Caesar is killed, Antony reveals that he is clever and cunning, especially when he speaks to the Roman people and wins them over to his point of view.

Even though Antony loved Caesar and was right to denounce the conspirators, there is a cruel and ruthless side to his nature. Unlike Brutus, his motives are not pure. He wants power for himself, as much as he wants to avenge Caesar's death.

Cassius

At the beginning of the play, Cassius is not a very likeable character. He is moody and quarrelsome and later takes bribes. He broods over things and does not seem to enjoy life.

But Cassius has good qualities, too. He understands people better than Brutus and he gives sensible advice about the battle which Brutus ignores. He loves his friends and is loyal to them, especially Brutus. In the end, we warm toward Cassius because he is really more 'human' than Brutus.

Portia

Portia

Portia, Brutus's wife, is noble and generous. Her father, Cato, was a famous Roman statesman and she is an educated woman. She is used to hearing about affairs of state, and when her husband does not confide in her, she is upset. When he does tell her about the conspiracy, it disturbs her. She prays for success but we feel that she knows he has taken the wrong course. When the enemies appear to be winning, her feelings get the better of her. She despairs and commits suicide rather than face dishonour.

Mark Antony

Cassius

MACBETH

Illustrations by Lesley Scoble

The story of Macbeth

Meeting the witches

Right at the beginning, Shakespeare sets the mood of the
story. There is thunder and lightning and three witches
appear. They announce that they will meet again on a heath
to greet Macbeth. Then they disappear into the 'filthy air' as
mysteriously as they arrived. What terrible things, the
audience wonders, will they say to Macbeth?

How brave Macbeth defeats the enemy

Meanwhile, a battle has been going on between soldiers
loyal to King Duncan of Scotland and the troops of some
rebel Scottish lords. The rebels have been supported in
battle by the King of Norway and his soldiers. But, after
fierce fights, Duncan's bravest and most loyal general, the
noble Macbeth, defeats the enemy. The King learns that one
of the rebel lords, the Thane of Cawdor, has been caught
and he orders that he be killed as a traitor. So pleased is the
King with Macbeth that he bestows on him the title Thane
of Cawdor. And he sends two of his noblemen, Ross and
Angus, to greet Macbeth – who is returning from battle –
with the news.

Macbeth and Banquo meet the witches

Macbeth is returning from the battle with his friend and
fellow nobleman, Banquo. Their journey back to the King's

camp takes them over a deserted heath. Here the witches lie in wait for them – talking as they do about the evil spells they have cast on people. The mist clears and Macbeth and Banquo suddenly see the witches. They demand that these creatures 'So wither'd and so wild in their attire', explain who they are. When the witches speak, they greet Macbeth as Thane of Cawdor and prophesy that he will be king. To Banquo they say, 'Your heirs will be kings, although you will not be king.' Then they disappear again. Puzzled and curious, Banquo and Macbeth do not know what to make of the incident.

Macbeth dreams of becoming king

At that moment Ross and Angus arrive. They tell Macbeth that he has been made Thane of Cawdor. Until then Macbeth did not know that Cawdor had been caught and killed. The first prophecy of the witches has come true. And Macbeth begins to think about the second one – that he will be king. Banquo warns him about evil spirits but Macbeth ponders aloud to himself. If, after all, he became Thane of Cawdor by chance, maybe he could also become king. For a moment, he imagines himself killing Duncan. Then he dismisses the horrid thought. We know though that he is now becoming ambitious.

Macbeth is honoured with the King's visit

At Duncan's castle, Macbeth and Banquo are warmly welcomed by the King. Duncan announces that he is making one of his sons, Malcolm, heir to the throne. Then he declares that he intends to visit Macbeth at his castle in Inverness. This is a great honour so Macbeth hurries off to prepare for the King's arrival. But as he leaves, he broods about Malcolm – the heir to the throne – and tries to suppress his own evil thoughts.

Lady Macbeth on Macbeth's nature
It is too full o' the milk of human kindness
To catch the nearest way: thou wouldst be great,
Art not without ambition, but without
The illness should attend it . . .

Act I Sc v

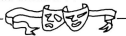

Lady Macbeth plans a murder

Meanwhile, at home in their castle in Inverness, Lady

Macbeth has received a letter from her husband. In it he tells her about the witches' prophecies.

At that moment a messenger arrives telling her of the King's visit. She realises that this is the golden opportunity to kill the King. She voices her treacherous thoughts to herself,

Lady Macbeth's determination to kill Duncan
The raven himself is hoarse
That croaks the fatal entrance of Duncan
Under my battlements. Come, you spirits
That tend on mortal thoughts! unsex me here,
And fill me from the crown to the toe top full
Of direst cruelty; make thick my blood,
Stop up the access and passage to remorse,
That no compunctious visitings of nature
Shake my fell purpose, nor keep peace between
The effect and it!

Act I Sc v

and unlike Macbeth does not try to suppress them. She makes up her mind that the murder must be committed that night. When Macbeth arrives at the castle ahead of the King, she tells him she has arranged everything.

Macbeth has his fears and doubts

Duncan arrives on a beautiful summer's day and Lady Macbeth welcomes him in a most friendly way. Macbeth, however, has been thinking about the murder. He is frightened about what will happen after he kills Duncan. He has doubts about it. Duncan is his cousin and he is a good king who is popular with everyone. Macbeth tells himself that there is no reason to kill Duncan – except to satisfy his own ambition to be king. So he tells Lady Macbeth that he has changed his mind.

Duncan describes Macbeth's castle
This castle hath a pleasant seat; the air
Nimbly and sweetly recommends itself
Unto our gentle senses

Act I Sc vi

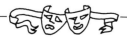

Lady Macbeth's anger

Lady Macbeth is furious. She accuses him of being a coward for not having the courage to do what he wants. She angrily says that she would kill her own child if that was what she had promised to do. Her feelings are so strong that Macbeth gives in completely. And he agrees to go ahead as she has planned.

Macbeth sees a blood-stained dagger

Banquo is also a guest at the castle. That night he feels uneasy and cannot sleep. He has been thinking of the witches and has a feeling that something terrible is going to happen. Macbeth, too, thinks about the murder. Alone in his room, he has a terrible vision of a dagger which he tries

Macbeth's vision of a dagger

Is this a dagger which I see before me,
The handle towards my hand? Come, let me clutch thee.
I have thee not, and yet I see thee still.
Art thou not, fatal vision, sensible
To feeling as to sight? or art thou but
A dagger of the mind, a false creation,
Proceeding from the heat-oppressed brain?

Act II Sc i

to grasp but cannot get hold of. He tells himself that he is imagining things because he is afraid. But he keeps seeing the dagger – the second time with blood on it. Then he hears a bell ring. This is Lady Macbeth's signal. He now has to kill Duncan.

Macbeth summoned to Duncan's murder

I go and it is done: the bell invites me.
Hear it not, Duncan, for it is a knell
That summons thee to heaven, or to hell.

Act II Sc i

How Macbeth murders Duncan

Lady Macbeth has made sure that Duncan's guards are asleep by putting drugs in their drink. And she has put out two daggers for Macbeth to use. She keeps watch outside

A disturbed night

The night has been unruly: where we lay,
Our chimneys were blown down, and, as they say,
Lamentings heard i' th' air, strange screams of death,
And prophesying with accents terrible
Of dire combustion and confused events...

Act II Sc iii

while Macbeth enters the King's chambers. When he comes out he is staggering. His arms are covered with blood and he is still holding the blood-stained daggers. It is obvious that Macbeth has gone to pieces. He is overcome by guilt and horror at what he has done. She tells him to pull himself together – to take the daggers back and smear the guards with blood. But Macbeth is in such a state of shock that he cannot. At that moment they hear a loud knocking at the gates of the castle. Lady Macbeth knows that this might awaken the household. She quickly replaces the daggers herself and sends Macbeth to change into his nightgown, so that he can pretend he has been asleep.

Macbeth on sleep

Methought I heard a voice cry 'Sleep no more!
Macbeth does murder sleep'– the innocent sleep,
Sleep that knits up the ravelled sleave of care,
The death of each day's life, sore labour's bath,
Balm of hurt minds, great Nature's second course,
Chief nourisher in life's feast, –

Act II Sc ii

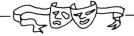

The horrible deed is discovered

The porter at the gate has been slow to open the gates. He had fallen into a drunken sleep and did not hear the knocking. Eventually he lets in the nobles, Lennox and Macduff. They explain to Macbeth that the King had asked them to call him at a very early hour. While Macduff goes to waken the King, Lennox describes how their night was disturbed by strange sounds and happenings. But just as he finishes speaking, Macduff returns horror stricken. He blurts out that Duncan has been murdered. He rings the alarm bells to wake up the castle while Macbeth rushes off to investigate. Lady Macbeth, Banquo and Duncan's sons hear the news as Macbeth returns. He confesses he has just killed the suspected murderers, the guards, in a fit of rage. Lady Macbeth faints – or pretends to faint – in horror.

Macbeth becomes King of Scotland

Confusion follows with no one knowing what to do. But Duncan's sons, Malcolm and Donalbain, think that if their father was killed, they too are in danger. They decide to flee. But this makes them suspects of the murder so Macbeth is appointed king – just as he wanted.

The new King plans another murder

Not long after he is crowned, Macbeth decides to give a banquet at his castle. He asks Banquo to be guest of honour. But Banquo secretly believes that Macbeth murdered Duncan. On the day of the banquet, Macbeth takes a special interest in how Banquo and his son Fleance are to spend the afternoon. The reason is that Macbeth is afraid of Banquo because of the witches' prophecy. They said, remember, that Banquo's heirs would be kings. In fact Macbeth has arranged to see some hired murderers who are to kill Banquo that afternoon – before the banquet.

Macbeth does not confide in the Queen

Lady Macbeth, meeting her husband after the murderers leave, thinks he is brooding about Duncan's murder. She tries to cheer him up by saying 'what's done, is done.' He asks her to be especially pleasant to Banquo that night. What he does not tell her is that he has already ordered the murder. And, sure enough, as Banquo and Fleance are returning to the castle for the banquet, they are attacked by the murderers. Banquo is killed but Fleance luckily escapes and runs away.

What happens at the banquet

Macbeth learns about Banquo's death and the escape of Fleance just as the banquet begins. Then, as he goes to take his place at the table, he sees the ghost of Banquo sitting in his seat. He is terrified and becomes disturbed. Lady Macbeth tries to explain his odd behaviour to the guests. He is not well, she says, and then quietly tells him to be sensible. He is imagining things. She believes it is better if the guests leave. When they do, Macbeth soon recovers. But he insists on seeing the witches again as soon as he can.

For Macbeth, there is no going back

. . . For mine own good
All causes shall give way: I am in blood
Stepped in so far that, should I wade no more
Returning were as tedious as go o'er.

Act III Sc iv

The witches foretell disaster

Macbeth finds the 'secret, black and midnight-hags' in a cave boiling up their witches' brew full of toads, snakes and other ghastly things. He demands that they tell him what is going to happen. They tell him to beware of Macduff. They say that no one 'of woman born' will harm Macbeth. Then they say he will not be defeated until 'Birnam wood comes to Dunsinane.' Macbeth is not too alarmed by these sayings. Anyway, he is convinced about the last one because forests and trees cannot move. Next he asks if Banquo's

heirs will be kings. He is shown a vision of eight kings –
which means that they will.

The witches' brew
Second Witch *Fillet of a fenny snake,*
In the cauldron boil and bake;
Eye of newt and toe of frog,
Wool of bat and tongue of dog,
Adder's fork and blind-worm's sting,
Lizard's leg and howlet's wing,
For a charm of powerful trouble,
Like a hell-broth boil and bubble.
All *Double, double toil and trouble;*
Fire burn and cauldron bubble.

Act IV Sc i

Macbeth's revenge on Macduff

Macbeth learns that Macduff has turned against him. He
has fled to England to join Malcolm who is organising an
army to march on Macbeth. In revenge he decides to kill
Macduff's family. Lady Macduff, who is upset that her
husband has hurried off to England, does not have time to
flee. She and her children are brutally murdered.

Malcolm tests Macduff's loyalty

In England Malcolm at first does not trust Macduff. He
thinks he could be a spy for Macbeth. So he tests his loyalty
by describing his own faults. Malcolm paints an evil picture
of himself and Macduff is shocked. Then Malcolm confesses he has lied; he just needed proof that Macduff was on his
side. Macduff now learns that his wife and family have been
killed by Macbeth. Grief stricken, he is determined to kill
Macbeth himself.

Lady Macbeth sleepwalks

Back in Scotland, Lady Macbeth is behaving oddly. Her
lady in waiting tells the doctor how her mistress sleepwalks.
They watch as she walks, talking to herself about Duncan's
murder and rubbing her hands. In her mind she describes
what happened and tries to wash the blood from her hands
over and over again. Her guilt has driven her mad.

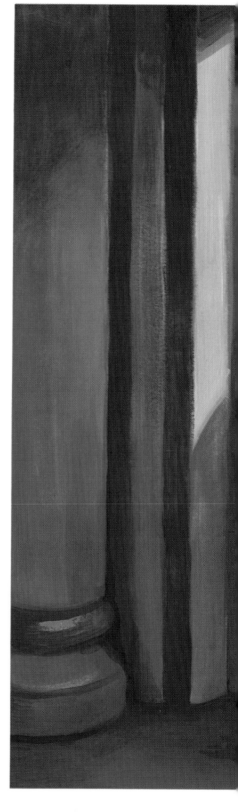

> **Lady Macbeth sleepwalking**
>
> *Out, damned spot! out, I say! . . . who would*
> *have thought the old man to have had so much blood in*
> *him? . . . What, will these hands ne'er be clean . . . Here's*
> *the smell of blood still: all the perfumes of Arabia*
> *will not sweeten this little hand . . .*

Act v Sc i

Macbeth prepares for battle

Macbeth, however, is busy setting up defences all around
Dunsinane Castle. Most of his noblemen and soldiers have
joined the other side. But he is certain he cannot be beaten –
or not until Birnam forest comes to Dunsinane.

What he does not know is that his enemies have agreed to
meet at Birnam wood. When the soldiers are gathered
there, each one is given the branch of a tree to camouflage
them as they move forward to attack. As he is preparing for
battle, Macbeth hears that Lady Macbeth has killed herself.
Now alone, he thinks how meaningless life is. Just then, a
messenger announces that Birnam wood appears to move.

> **Macbeth on how meaningless life is**
>
> *To-morrow, and to-morrow, and to-morrow,*
> *Creeps in this petty pace from day to day,*
> *To the last syllable of recorded time;*
> *And all our yesterdays have lighted fools*
> *The way to dusty death. Out, out, brief candle!*
> *Life's but a walking shadow, a poor player*
> *That struts and frets his hour upon the stage,*
> *And then is heard no more: it is a tale*
> *Told by an idiot, full of sound and fury,*
> *Signifying nothing.*

Act v Sc v

When Birnam wood meets Dunsinane

Malcolm and Macduff have begun their attack. And for
Macbeth, the witches' prophecy has come true. Macbeth
fights bravely but his castle is taken. He meets Macduff on
the battlefield but still believes he cannot be killed by a man
'of woman born'. But Macduff reveals that he was born
prematurely by Caesarian – so he was not born in the
normal way. And in their fight Macbeth is killed. Now at
last peace is restored to Scotland and the rightful heir,
Malcolm, is crowned king.

Characters in Macbeth

Macbeth

Macbeth is one of the most complicated of Shakespeare's characters. In describing him, Shakespeare shows how well he understands how different people think and act – and how a person can be driven to evil deeds by hidden ambitions and emotions within themselves.

At the beginning of the play, we learn that Macbeth is a brave soldier and a good man. He has proved his loyalty to King Duncan by defeating the enemy. Only after he meets the witches does he begin to think evil thoughts. But, being a good man, at first he does not give in to these.

Lady Macbeth knows her husband's nature better than most other people. She knows that deep down he wants to be king, just as the witches prophesied. But she thinks he is too weak willed to do anything about it. She realises that she must be the person who urges him to kill Duncan.

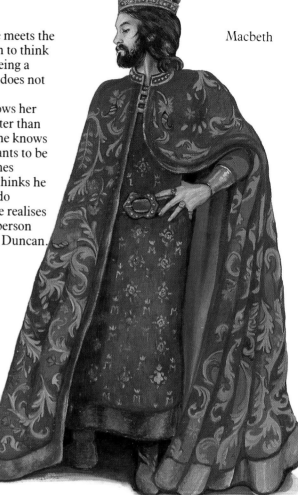

Macbeth

Lady Macbeth

Macduff's description of Macbeth

. . . Not in the legions
Of horrid hell can come a devil
more damned
In evils to top Macbeth

Act IV Sc iii

And she does. This shows how easily swayed Macbeth is, as does his listening to the witches in the first place.

Macbeth is not so worried about the wrong he is doing until after he has killed Duncan. Then he feels guilty and troubled by his conscience. He is in such a state of shock that he thinks he hears voices saying he has murdered sleep. But he soon puts these fears aside and pulls himself together.

When he becomes king, the evil side of his nature takes over completely. He becomes a butcher and a tyrant without any feelings of remorse. He

Lady Macbeth's accusation of cowardice

. . . Would'st thou have that
Which thou esteem'st the ornament of life,
And live a coward in thine own esteem,
Letting 'I dare not' wait upon 'I would'

Act I Sc vii

Macbeth's ambitions

Macbeth . . . Stars, hide your
* fires!*
Let not light see my black and
* deep desires . . .*

Act I Sc iv

plans the murder of Banquo in the most cold-blooded way. Before, he had to be persuaded by his wife to kill. Now, he does not even bother to tell her of his plans. We do get one glimpse of the cowardly side of his nature at the banquet when he is disturbed by the vision of Banquo's ghost. But as before, the feeling of fear and guilt soon passes. By now, he knows that he has given in to the evil.

Macbeth on the murder of Duncan

If it were done, when 'tis done,
* then 'twere well*
It were done quickly:

Act I Sc vii

He callously orders the brutal murder of Lady Macduff and her children even though they can do him no harm. Even when his wife goes mad, he does not show much concern. He trusts completely in the witches' prophecies. Although he is deserted by his soldiers and hated by everyone, he really believes he cannot be defeated.

Only when his wife commits suicide does he show some feeling. Then we see what kind

of man he might have been had he not given in to evil. And just for a moment we feel sorry for him, as he thinks about how meaningless his life is – and about his hopes for a happy old age. His spirit is broken but he is determined to carry on. And in the end he dies bravely. What is tragic in this story, Shakespeare tells us, is that here was a good, honest and honourable man who allowed himself to be totally corrupted by evil ambitions.

No comfortable old age for Macbeth

. . . that which should
* accompany old age,*
As honour, love, obedience,
* troops of friends,*
I must not look to have

Act V Sc iii

Lady Macbeth

Shakespeare deliberately creates a contrast between the nature of Lady Macbeth and her husband. At the beginning of the play, she is the strong-willed, ambitious person. It is Macbeth who is weak and uncertain. But, like Macbeth, Shakespeare shows us how her character is affected by the murders of Duncan and Banquo so that she goes mad and commits suicide.

Lady Macbeth is more ambitious for her husband than he is. She imagines a wonderful future for him as king. Only for a moment does she stop to think if it is right or wrong to

kill Duncan. She expresses her feelings so strongly that Macbeth – who is rather a weak person – totally gives in to her wishes. She is also a sensible and practical woman. She plans the details of the murder. And she drugs the guards and puts out the daggers. When Macbeth is too shaken to return the daggers after the murder, she does it.

She, then, is the wicked woman who goads Macbeth into murdering Duncan. Without her Macbeth might not have translated the temptation to murder into the

Duncan

Lady Macbeth dismisses failure

We fail?
But screw your courage to the sticking-place,
And we'll not fail . . .

Act I Sc vi

actual deed. Remember, though, that Lady Macbeth is not only ambitious for herself – but also for Macbeth. In this respect, she is a good wife who supports her husband's plans for getting on in the world. She is a charming hostess to Duncan and later at the banquet apologises for Macbeth's strange behaviour. She is self-confident and calm whenever Macbeth panics or imagines things. She knows Macbeth's weak points. And she uses her own strong nature to supply the courage he does not have. (In other circumstances, you might almost admire her tremendous determination to get for Macbeth what he wants.) She certainly cannot count on her husband when her courage deserts her. Once Macbeth becomes king he does not need his wife's support. It is as if her strength of character has been taken over by him – and his weaknesses by her.

She is now the person who broods about the dreadful things they have done. She is frightened of the dark. She walks in her sleep and washes her hands all the time to get rid of the blood. Her guilty conscience drives her mad and she commits suicide.

Duncan

Shakespeare uses the character of Duncan to make a contrast with Macbeth. While Macbeth is a traitor, Duncan is honest, humble and good. He shows he has a generous nature by praising Macbeth so warmly and by giving Lady Macbeth the present of a diamond. Popular with his subjects, he ruled fairly and wisely. By murdering him, Shakespeare tells us, Macbeth murdered an ideal king.

Banquo

Like Macbeth, Banquo is a brave and loyal soldier. When he is with Macbeth and the witches he too is given a prophecy. But he recognises that the witches are evil creatures and he resists their temptations. He is an honest and trusting man and he does not suspect Macbeth until it is too late. In a way, Banquo is the hero of the play. Whereas Macbeth gives in to evil thoughts and ambitions, Banquo does not. And this, Shakespeare is telling us, is how Macbeth should have acted.

Macduff

Macduff is suspicious of Macbeth straight after Duncan's murder. Like Banquo, he is a straightforward, honest man. He firmly believes that the tyrant Macbeth must be destroyed and the rightful king, Malcolm, put on the throne. He is a man of action and goes to England to join Malcolm. But this brave act causes the death of his unprotected wife and children. He gets his revenge, however, by killing Macbeth and helping to restore peace to Scotland.

Banquo   Macduff

HAMLET

Illustrations by Roger Payne

The story of Hamlet

The guards of Elsinore Castle in Denmark have seen a Ghost on the battlements. It looks like the father of Prince Hamlet who died only two months before. They ask Horatio, a young nobleman and a friend of the Prince, to watch with them and to talk to the Ghost. When it appears, it does not speak, and disappears from sight.

The new King of Denmark

The new King of Denmark is Claudius, Hamlet's uncle who has just married the Prince's mother, Gertrude. He allows Laertes, the son of his Lord Chamberlain, Polonius, to return to Paris and urges Hamlet to cast off his mourning.

Hamlet is still distressed by his father's death and deeply upset that his mother has married barely two months afterwards. He longs for death and condemns his mother with the words, 'Frailty, thy name is woman.'

Hamlet's longing for death
O! that this too too solid flesh would melt,
Thaw and resolve itself into a dew . . .
How weary, stale, flat, and unprofitable
Seem to me all the uses of this world.

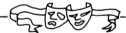

Act I Sc ii

Polonius bids farewell to his son, advising him on how a young man should behave.

Polonius's advice to his son
Neither a borrower, nor a lender be;
For loan oft loses both itself and friend,
And borrowing dulls the edge of husbandry.
This above all: to thine own self be true,
And it must follow, as the night the day,
Thou canst not then be false to any man.

Act I Sc iii

A ghostly meeting

Hamlet, meanwhile, has gone to the castle battlements with Horatio. When the Ghost appears, he speaks to Hamlet, as the spirit of his dead father. The Ghost tells how he was

murdered by Claudius and asks Hamlet to revenge his
death. Hamlet asks Horatio to keep the meeting secret
saying, 'There are more things in heaven and earth,
Horatio, Than are dreamt of in your philosophy.'

Hamlet feigns madness

Hamlet decides to find proof of his uncle's wickedness. He is determined to kill the King, and pretends to be mad in order to trick him. Ophelia, Laertes' sister, who has been courted by Hamlet, notices his strange behaviour. She tells her father, Polonius, who decides that Hamlet is lovesick for Ophelia.

Claudius, the King, is also worried about Hamlet's behaviour. He sends for Rosencrantz and Guildenstern, old school friends of Hamlet, and asks if they can find out what is wrong with him.

Hamlet soon discovers that they are messengers from the King. He describes his melancholy to them.

Hamlet's melancholy

I have of late, – but wherefore I know not, – lost all my mirth, forgone all custom of exercises; and indeed it goes so heavily with my disposition that this goodly frame, the earth, seems to me a sterile promontory; this most excellent canopy, the air, look you, this brave o'erhanging firmament, this majestical roof fretted with golden fire, why, it appears no other thing to me but a foul and pestilent congregation of vapours. What a piece of work is a man! How noble in reason! how infinite in faculty! in form, in moving, how express and admirable! in action how like an angel! in apprehension how like a god! the beauty of the world! the paragon of animals! And yet, to me, what is this quintessence of dust?

Act II Sc ii

Hamlet's plot to trick the King

Hamlet learns that a group of travelling players are to perform at Elsinore Castle. Hamlet asks the actors if they will add a scene to their play – it resembles the way in which his father was murdered. If Claudius reacts to the scene on stage, Hamlet will know that the King is guilty. He says to himself, '. . . The play's the thing, Wherein I'll catch the conscience of the king.'

Hamlet spurns Ophelia

The King and Queen decide to see if Hamlet is suffering from lovesickness. They arrange for Ophelia to be alone with Hamlet, but where the King and Polonius can eavesdrop on the conversation. Hamlet ponders on death and asks whether it is better to live or die.

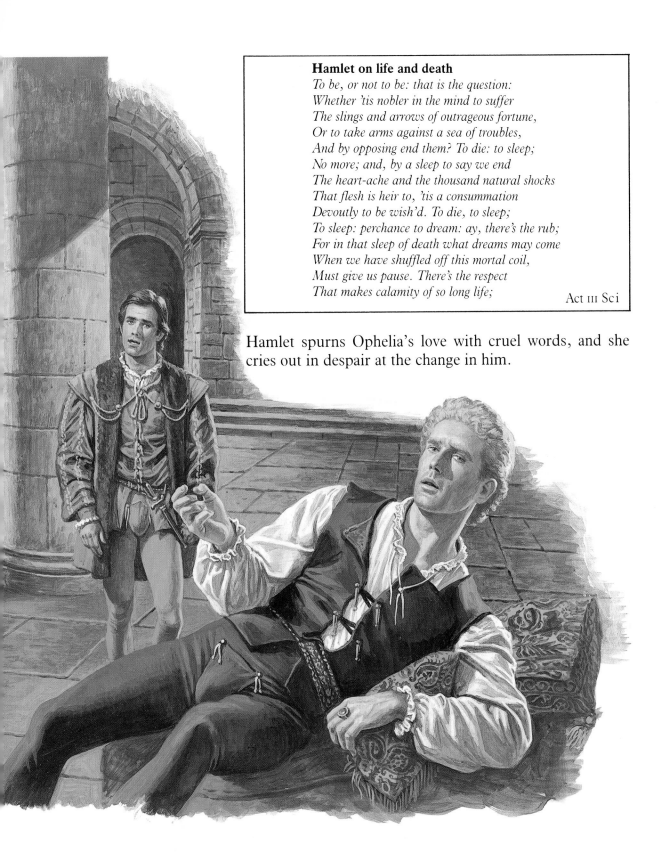

Hamlet on life and death

To be, or not to be: that is the question:
Whether 'tis nobler in the mind to suffer
The slings and arrows of outrageous fortune,
Or to take arms against a sea of troubles,
And by opposing end them? To die: to sleep;
No more; and, by a sleep to say we end
The heart-ache and the thousand natural shocks
That flesh is heir to, 'tis a consummation
Devoutly to be wish'd. To die, to sleep;
To sleep: perchance to dream: ay, there's the rub;
For in that sleep of death what dreams may come
When we have shuffled off this mortal coil,
Must give us pause. There's the respect
That makes calamity of so long life;

Act III Sc i

Hamlet spurns Ophelia's love with cruel words, and she cries out in despair at the change in him.

Hamlet rejects Ophelia

. . . Get thee to a nunnery, go; farewell. Or, if thou wilt needs marry, marry a fool; for wise men know well enough what monsters you make of them. To a nunnery, go; and quickly too. Farewell.

Act III Sci

The King now knows that it is not love that disturbs Hamlet. He suspects Hamlet of evil plans and decides to send him to England.

The play's the thing

Before the play takes place in front of the court, Hamlet advises the actors on how to play their parts.

Hamlet's instructions to the players

Suit the action to the word, the word to the action; with this special observance, that you o'erstep not the modesty of nature; for anything so overdone is from the purpose of playing, whose end, both at the first and now, was and is, to hold, as 'twere, the mirror up to nature; to show virtue her own feature, scorn her own image, and the very age and body of the time his form and pressure. Now, this overdone, or come tardy off, though it make the unskilful laugh, cannot but make the judicious grieve ... O! there be players that I have seen play, and heard others praise ... that I have thought some of nature's journeymen had made men and not made them well, they imitated humanity so abominably.

Act III Sc i

Hamlet carefully watches the reactions of Claudius and his mother to the play. 'The lady doth protest too much, methinks,' is Gertrude's response, but the King is disturbed. When the actors reach the point where the Player King is poisoned, Claudius stops the play. Frightened and guilty, he rushes from the hall. Hamlet is now convinced that Claudius murdered his father and he is determined on revenge.

Hamlet's thoughts on revenge

'Tis now the very witching time of night,
When churchyards yawn and hell itself breathes out
Contagion to this world: now could I drink hot blood,
And do such bitter business as the day
Would quake to look on.

Act III Sc ii

A chance to kill the King

The King now realises that Hamlet knows of his murderous deed. Alone, Claudius tries to pray for forgiveness but finds it difficult. Hamlet, seeing him alone, rejects the chance to kill him. If the King's prayers were heard, argues Hamlet to himself, Claudius might be forgiven and would not suffer the fires of hell.

Polonius behind the arras

Hamlet has been summoned to see his mother and she agrees that Polonius should hide behind the arras, or tapestry curtain, to listen to their conversation. Hamlet speaks harshly to his mother, threatening her, and Polonius cries out, alarmed for her safety. Hamlet, believing it to be the King, draws his sword and thrusts it through the curtain. Polonius falls dead at his feet.

The Queen, convinced that her son is mad, tells the King of Polonius's death. Claudius knows that the blow was intended for him and insists that Hamlet leave for England at once.

Ophelia's madness

Soon after Hamlet sets out for England, it becomes obvious that Ophelia has gone mad because of her father's death and the loss of Hamlet's love. 'When sorrows come, they come not single spies, But in battalions,' observes Claudius.

> **Ophelia's lament**
> *He is dead and gone, lady,*
> *He is dead and gone;*
> *At his head a grass-green turf,*
> *At his heels a stone.*
> Act IV Sc v

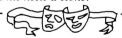

Laertes, who has heard of his father's death, rushes back to Denmark. He is shocked by Ophelia's insanity. She strews flowers and sings, oblivious of her surroundings.

> **Ophelia's madness**
> *There's rosemary, that's for remembrance; pray, love, remember: and there is pansies, that's for thoughts ... There's fennel for you, and columbines; there's rue for you; and here's some for me; we may call it herb of grace o'Sundays. O! you must wear your rue with a difference. There's a daisy; I would give you some violets, but they withered all when my father died.*
> Act IV Sc v

Claudius urges Laertes to revenge

Claudius convinces Laertes that Hamlet is responsible for Polonius's death and also for Ophelia's madness. When they learn from a messenger that Hamlet has not gone to England but is returning to court, they set up a plan to kill him.

Claudius advises Laertes to challenge Hamlet to a fencing match. Laertes agrees but says that he will add poison to the tip of the sword. To make sure that Hamlet dies, Claudius decides to add poison to the wine Hamlet will drink during the duel.

The death of Ophelia

When the Queen informs them that Ophelia has died by drowning, Laertes is even more intent on revenge.

Ophelia's death

There is a willow grows aslant a brook,
That shows his hoar leaves in the glassy stream;
There with fantastic garlands did she come,
Of crow-flowers, nettles, daisies, and long purples,
That liberal shepherds give a grosser name,
But our cold maids do dead men's fingers call them:
There, on the pendent boughs her coronet weeds
Clambering to hang, an envious sliver broke,
When down her weedy trophies and herself
Fell in the weeping brook. Her clothes spread wide,
And, mermaid-like, awhile they bore her up;
Which time she chanted snatches of old tunes,
As one incapable of her own distress,
Or like a creature native and indu'd
Unto that element; but long it could not be
Till that her garments, heavy with their drink,
Pull'd the poor wretch from her melodious lay
To muddy death.

Act IV Sc vii

At the graveyard

Hamlet on his return to Elsinore has been met by Horatio in the graveyard outside the city. Here the grave diggers are preparing a fresh grave. Hamlet talks to the grave diggers and learns that one of the skulls dug up is that of his father's court jester, Yorick. It reminds him of happier times.

Hamlet remembers Yorick

Alas! poor Yorick. I knew him, Horatio; a fellow of infinite jest, of most excellent fancy; he hath borne me on his back a thousand times; and now ... Where be your gibes now? your gambols? your songs? your flashes of merriment, that were wont to set the table on a roar? Not one now, to mock your own grinning?

Act v Sc i

123

Horatio and Hamlet discover that the grave is for Ophelia. Hamlet declares his love for Ophelia, but Laertes insists that the fencing match take place.

The fatal duel

The fencing match begins, but during it there is a scuffle and both Hamlet and Laertes are cut with the poisoned sword. The Queen picks up the wine meant for Hamlet, and before the King can stop her, she drinks it and she dies. Hamlet picks up the poisoned sword and kills the King.

Hamlet's death

Laertes dies and it is clear that Hamlet, too, is dying. Horatio wants to drink the poisoned wine in order to die with Hamlet, but Hamlet insists that he remain alive to tell Hamlet's story and clear his name.

Before he dies, Hamlet appoints the young Norwegian prince, Fortinbras, as his successor to the throne. As Hamlet dies in Horatio's arms, Horatio bids him a last farewell.

At that moment, Fortinbras arrives at the Danish court from Poland to find a scene of devastation. The play ends with a tribute to Hamlet by Fortinbras.

> **Horatio's farewell**
> *. . . Good-night, sweet prince,*
> *And flights of angels sing thee to thy rest!*
>
> ACT V Sc ii

Characters in Hamlet

Hamlet

Hamlet

Hamlet is one of the most complicated of all Shakespeare's characters. Sometimes he is gentle and thoughtful, but on numerous occasions throughout the play he is cruel and bitter – especially with his mother and Ophelia. Although we see him as a sensitive person who thinks deeply about the meaning of life, he is also a man of action. He plans and carries out his revenge quite ruthlessly, pretending he is mad in order to achieve his ends. Hamlet's behaviour is often odd and uncontrolled, and he even apologises to Laertes for being 'punished, With sore distraction', blaming his 'madness.' He seems to have violent swings of mood. He is brave in battle, honest and forthright. He is a loyal and honourable man who, according to Fortinbras, would have made a good ruler. He is an intriguing character. Was he really mad? Or was he only pretending? His cruelty to Ophelia and his unfeeling response to the death of Polonius can, perhaps, be excused if he was mad. Hamlet is not an easy person to understand, and many experts have tried to explain his contradictory behaviour. This is why he is one of the most interesting characters ever created by Shakespeare.

Ophelia

Ophelia is beautiful, kind and gentle. She is an innocent girl and a dutiful and loving daughter, who is willing to follow her father's advice. When, however, she meets Hamlet there is no doubt that she loves him deeply. When Hamlet rejects her love, she cries out in despair at the change in him, pitying herself as well as him. Ophelia's madness is caused by Hamlet's rejection, and by the death of her father. She becomes a pathetic creature who wears flowers and sings songs about the loss of a loved one. She simply cannot endure the suffering that has befallen her.

Polonius

Thou wretched, rash, intruding fool

Polonius is an old man but a responsible member of the King's household. He is the father of Laertes and Ophelia. He loves talking to anyone who is willing to listen to him, but Hamlet regards him as an old fool. Although he talks too much, as many old people do, some of his words are wise. His advice on how a gentleman should behave and dress is very sensible. He says, 'Costly thy habit as thy purse can buy, But not express'd in fancy: rich, not gaudy; For the apparel oft proclaims the man.'

Ophelia on Hamlet's nature
O! What a noble mind is here o'erthrown:
The courtier's, soldier's, scholar's, eye, tongue, sword;
The expectancy and rose of the fair state,
The glass of fashion and the mould of form,
The observ'd of all observers . . .

Act III Sc i

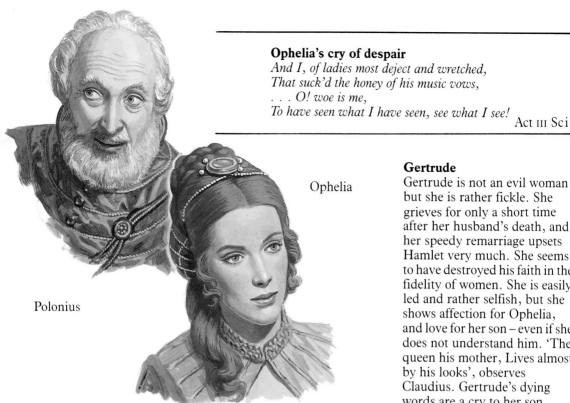

Polonius

Ophelia

Ophelia's cry of despair
And I, of ladies most deject and wretched,
That suck'd the honey of his music vows,
. . . O! woe is me,
To have seen what I have seen, see what I see!

Act III Sc i

Gertrude

Gertrude is not an evil woman but she is rather fickle. She grieves for only a short time after her husband's death, and her speedy remarriage upsets Hamlet very much. She seems to have destroyed his faith in the fidelity of women. She is easily led and rather selfish, but she shows affection for Ophelia, and love for her son – even if she does not understand him. 'The queen his mother, Lives almost by his looks', observes Claudius. Gertrude's dying words are a cry to her son.

Claudius

O! my offence is rank, it smells to heaven; It hath the primal eldest curse upon't; A brother's murder!

Claudius killed his brother because he wanted to be King, and to marry his brother's wife. He is an evil man who is prepared to murder Hamlet in order to keep his throne. But like most of Shakespeare's villains, he is not totally wicked; he does feel remorse and guilt for what he has done. He tries to pray for forgiveness but knows that it is useless. He feels sympathy for the mad Ophelia but his human qualities are outweighed by his evil ones. He is the person who is the cause of the play's tragedy.

Claudius

Gertrude

The King's love for Gertrude
She's so conjunctive to my life and soul,
That, as the star moves not but in his sphere,
I could not but by her.

126

KING LEAR

Illustrations by Gwen Green

The story of King Lear

All the lords of Britain are gathered to hear the ageing King Lear's future plans. The earls of Gloucester and Kent are speculating about what he will say. Gloucester introduces Edmund, his illegitimate son, to Kent. The bustling court falls silent as Lear enters with his daughters, Goneril, Regan and Cordelia, and the husbands of the elder two.

Lear speaks: today he will divide his kingdom amongst his daughters, and say which of Cordelia's two suitors may marry her. Each daughter will get a portion of land according to how much she loves her father.

Words of love

Goneril, the eldest, swears she loves her father 'dearer than eyesight, space and liberty'. Lear offers her a good share of his kingdom. Regan agrees with her sister – except, she says, that Goneril has not gone far enough. She too is assured of her share. Cordelia, the youngest, wonders what she can say in return.

Lear calls Cordelia to declare her love. What can she say to outshine the others? 'Nothing, my lord,' she replies. Lear, aghast, asks her to speak again. Cordelia protests that true love cannot be put into fine words.

Angrily, Lear declares that Cordelia will get nothing. The Earl of Kent interrupts, begging him to see sense. But the stubborn old king orders him to leave his kingdom.

Lear asks Cordelia's suitors if either will marry her, now she is a pauper, not a princess. The Duke of Burgundy refuses; but the King of France gladly offers his hand to her. Cordelia says a tearful goodbye to her sisters, who treat her scornfully. When she has gone, they reveal their true feelings: they think their father is a fool, and neither will put up with his changeable moods for long. Neither looks forward to his plan of staying alternate months with them.

A wicked son

Edmund, too, plans to deceive his father. He is resentful because, as a younger son and illegitimate, he will not inherit Gloucester's land. He has a plan to turn Gloucester against his legitimate brother, Edgar.

The old earl comes in, muttering about the strange events at court. Edmund hastily stuffs a letter into his pocket.

Cordelia's love

> Good my lord,
> You have begot me, bred me, lov'd me: I
> Return those duties back as are right fit,
> Obey you, love you, and most honour you.
> Why have my sisters husbands, if they say
> They love you all? Haply, when I shall wed,
> That lord whose hand must take my plight shall carry
> Half my love with him, half my care and duty:
> Sure I shall never marry like my sisters,
> To love my father all.
>
> Act I Sc i

Gloucester asks to see it. His son appears reluctant, but hands it over. It complains that old men are tyrants, who deny their sons money and power until they too are too old to enjoy them, and hints at a conspiracy against Gloucester; and it is signed 'Edgar'. The horrified Gloucester does not suspect the truth, which is that Edmund has forged the letter. He blames everything on 'these late eclipses of the sun and moon'.

Edmund has no time for eclipses and astrology; he believes that people make their own fate. When he sees Edgar, he asks him what he has done to offend Gloucester. Edgar is puzzled; they have not quarrelled. Edmund advises him to run away, and make sure to carry a weapon with him.

Kent's loyalty

Lear is staying with Goneril and her husband, the Duke of Albany. Already there is friction. The old king has struck a courtier for telling off his Fool. The hundred personal knights that accompany the king are troublesome and expensive to keep. Goneril tells Oswald, her steward, to treat Lear badly, hoping to drive him away to stay with Regan.

Kent disguises himself as a poor man, and persuades Lear to hire him as a servant. He soon gains the king's favour, and a tip, by tripping up the insolent Oswald.

The Fool

In comes Lear's Fool – the only person the old king will accept criticism from. He makes his points in jokes and riddles. Seeing Lear tipping Kent, the Fool offers the new servant his court jester's cap. He explains that Kent must be a fool to follow a fool like Lear.

'Dost thou call me fool, boy?' asks Lear. Yes, says the Fool: 'All other titles hast thou given away; that thou wast born with.'

Goneril tells Lear to dismiss fifty knights. Enraged, Lear sets off at once to stay with Regan. Goneril sends Oswald ahead, to warn her sister that he is coming.

Edmund's plot

Lear sends Kent to Regan with his side of the story. At once Regan and her husband, the Duke of Cornwall, ride to Gloucester's castle, to ask for his advice. They take Kent and Oswald with them to await their replies.

At the castle, Edmund warns Edgar, who has been hiding, to flee, not just from his father but from Cornwall, too. He pretends to believe that Edgar has made an enemy of Cornwall. Suddenly the brothers hear Gloucester arrive. Edgar runs away into the night. Edmund cuts his own arm with his sword so that he can pretend that Edgar has attacked and wounded him.

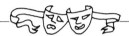

Edmund tells his father that Edgar was planning to kill him. Gloucester says he will bestow his lands on Edmund.

Regan, Cornwall and their party arrive. While the nobles discuss what to do about Lear, Kent and Oswald meet and quarrel bitterly. The argument turns into a fight. Cornwall intervenes and puts Kent into the stocks – a grave insult to his royal master.

> **Kent insults the villainous Oswald**
> *A knave, a rascal, an eater of broken meats; a base, proud, shallow, beggarly, three-suited, hundred-pound, filthy, worsted-stocking knave; a lily-liver'd, action-taking knave; a whoreson, glass-gazing, superserviceable, finical rogue; one-trunk-inheriting slave; one that wouldst be a bawd, in way of good service, and art nothing but the composition of a knave, beggar, coward, pandar, and the son and heir of a mongrel bitch: one whom I will beat into clamorous whining if thou deniest the least syllable of thy addition.*
>
> Act II Sc ii

Kent is secretly glad to be alone in the stocks; it gives him a chance to read a letter from Cordelia. She and the King of France have plans.

Lear dispossessed

Lear and the Fool arrive at Regan's palace, to find nobody home. They proceed to Gloucester's castle, and find Kent in the stocks. Lear is outraged at this new insult, and even more by his daughter's refusal to let him in.

Gloucester brings Regan and Cornwall out, and Kent is released. Lear greets Regan kindly, and starts to tell her how Goneril has mistreated him. She cuts him short, saying her sister was in the right and telling him to go back and beg forgiveness. Then Goneril herself arrives.

'Art not ashamed to look upon this beard?' asks Lear. Though Regan greets her sister warmly, the king still believes she will take him, hundred knights and all. As they talk, however, the number of knights each will accept falls. Regan says she can take only twenty-five – so Lear says he will go with Goneril, who will let him have fifty. But Goneril says he does not need any knights at all – there are plenty of servants at her palace.

Crying for revenge, Lear walks out. A terrible storm is brewing, but his daughters do not try to stop him.

Kent and the Fool are the only followers Lear has left. Kent sends a messenger to Cordelia, who has secretly landed at Dover with the King of France's army.

The blasted heath

Lear and his two loyal servants wander over a lonely heath.

> **How many knights?**
> Gon. *Hear me, my lord. What need you five-and-twenty, ten, or five, To follow in a house, where twice so many Have a command to tend you?*
> Reg. *What need one?*
> Lear. *O! reason not the need; our basest beggars Are in the poorest thing superfluous: Allow not nature more than nature needs, Man's life is cheap as beast's.*
>
> Act II Sc iv

Lear defies the storm

*Blow, winds, and crack
your cheeks! rage! blow!
You cataracts and
hurricanoes, spout
Till you have drench'd our
steeples, drown'd the
cocks!*

Act III Sc iii

The old king shouts defiantly at the thunder and lightning; cruel as they are, they are not as bad as his ungrateful daughters. He is losing his mind. Kent gently leads his master to the shelter of a tiny hovel.

Gloucester in exile

Regan turns Gloucester out of his own home, for trying to defend the king. He complains of this to Edmund, and mentions a letter he has received, telling him of the French invasion. Deciding to join the king, he asks Edmund to deceive Cornwall about his plans. Edmund sees a path to power for himself. He will betray his father and tell Cornwall about the invasion.

A strange new friend

On the heath, Lear sends the Fool into the hovel. The Fool runs out, terrified of a 'spirit' inside. Its name is Poor Tom, he says – the country name for a madman.

But 'Poor Tom' is not what he seems; he is Edgar, in disguise. He shouts crazily about a foul fiend that is plaguing him. Lear, obsessed with his own troubles, asks if 'Tom's' daughters have driven him mad – what else could bring a man so low?

Gloucester arrives with a flaming torch, to take Lear and his friends to safety. He does not recognise Edgar, who pretends to mistake him for the fiend. Lear wants to go on talking to the madman, whose ravings seem to him like profound philosophy, but at last Gloucester leads them to an outhouse of his castle where they can hide.

There, Lear decides to try his daughters for treason. His followers – the Fool, Edgar and Kent – sit like a bench of magistrates. Stools take the place of the accused.

Kent is so upset by his old master's sad, crazed manner, that he begins to cry. Gloucester, who knows the old king's life is in danger, tells Kent to take Lear to Dover.

Cordelia will protect him there.

Gloucester is blinded

Inside the castle, news of the French invasion has arrived – and the hunt is on for Gloucester. Goneril, Edmund and Oswald set off to take the news to Albany.

Gloucester is soon caught. Regan and Cornwall question him harshly. When Gloucester says he cannot bear to see the treatment meted out to Lear, Cornwall cruelly crushes one

Lear's newfound compassion

*Poor naked wretches,
  wheresoe'er you are,
That bide the pelting of this
  pitiless storm,
How shall your houseless
  heads and unfed sides,
Your loop'd and window'd
  raggedness, defend you
From seasons such as these?
O! I have ta'en
Too little care of this.*

Act III Sc iv

Cornwall's cruelty

*. . . but I shall see
The winged vengeance
  overtake such children.*
Corn. *See't shalt thou
  never. Fellows, hold the
  chair.*
*Upon these eyes of thine I'll
  set my foot.*
Glo. *He that will think
  to live till he be old,
Give me some help! O
  cruel! O ye gods!*

Act III Sc vii

of his eyes. Shocked by this barbarity, one of the servants attacks his master, but Regan kills him. Though gravely wounded, Cornwall has enough strength to put out Gloucester's other eye. The old man is led away, blood pouring down his face. The other servants, deserting their evil lord, bind Gloucester's wounds with flax and egg-white.

On the heath, Edgar (still disguised as 'Poor Tom') sees Gloucester coming. Gloucester asks the servant leading him to leave him with the madman. He offers 'Tom' money to take him to the cliffs of Dover.

A faithless wife

Goneril and Edmund arrive at Albany's palace, to learn that he welcomes the French invasion. He hates Goneril's cruelty to her father. Goneril sends Edmund back to Regan with this news – giving him a passionate kiss. She loves the vicious Edmund far more than the husband she now despises.

Albany comes in and expresses his disgust for Goneril's attitude. A messenger brings the news that Cornwall is dead; the servant's wound proved fatal after all. Hearing how Gloucester was blinded, Albany swears to avenge him.

Summons to arms

Cordelia now knows her father's fate. Both sad and angry, she asks a doctor if his madness can be cured. First, however, she must defeat Goneril and Regan.

The two sisters are no longer friends. Regan, now a widow, means to marry Edmund, but knows Goneril loves him too. She uses Oswald in a plan to outwit her sister. At the same time, she regrets letting Gloucester live and callously proposes that Oswald 'cuts him off', if he finds him.

A leap in the dark

Gloucester himself wants to die. As they approach Dover, he asks Edgar how much further it is to the cliff-top. Edgar tells him they are nearly there; can he not hear the sea? Gloucester cannot. He is puzzled – the madman seems different. He no longer babbles about foul fiends, but talks calmly. Edgar says they have reached the edge of the cliff; it makes him dizzy to look down.

Gloucester sends 'Tom' away. Then he jumps.

Miraculous rescue?

But his fall does not kill him. A friendly stranger helps him

A fearful precipice
*How fearful
And dizzy 'tis to cast one's
eyes so low!
The crows and choughs that
wing the midway air
Show scarce so gross as
beetles; half way down
Hangs one that gathers
samphire, dreadful
trade!
Methinks he seems no bigger
than his head.
The fishermen that walk
upon the beach
Appear like mice, and yond
tall anchoring bark
Diminish'd to her cock, her
cock a buoy
Almost too small for sight.*
Act IV Sc vi

up, exclaiming about his miraculous survival. The stranger asks who it was that he saw with Gloucester on the cliff-top. 'A poor unfortunate beggar,' answers the old man. The stranger says it looked to him like a demon with horns. The gods have saved the old man from hell. Gloucester remembers how 'Poor Tom' talked of devils and fiends. He resolves to bear his troubles in future.

But the stranger is really Edgar. He led his father to the top of a little knoll, pretending it was the cliff, and cleverly prevented him from taking his own life.

Mad Lear

As they talk, Lear comes by, raving. Gloucester knows his voice and kneels to kiss his hand. Lear mistakes him for the blind god of love, Cupid. He shouts about the world's wickedness and lustfulness.

At last Lear recognises Gloucester. In his ravings, he talks of killing his enemies. Then a group of men appear, saying they have come from his 'most dear daughter'. Thinking they are from Goneril or Regan, he runs away, and they chase after him. It was Cordelia who sent them, as Gloucester and Edgar realise.

Cordelia's kindness
Mine enemy's dog,
Though he had bit me,
should have stood that
night
Against my fire. And wast
though fain, poor father,
To hovel thee with swine
and rogues forlorn,
In short and musty straw!
Alack, alack!

Act IV Sc vii

As the pair set off towards Cordelia's camp, Oswald enters. He draws his sword, but Edgar fights and kills him. As he dies, Oswald orders Edgar – not knowing who he is – to give a letter he has from Goneril to Edmund. The letter asks Edmund to kill Albany.

Lear and Cordelia reunited

At the camp, Lear is now safely asleep. Cordelia goes to see him and wakes him with a kiss. At first Lear does not believe it is her; he is overjoyed when he does.

The armies meet

Edmund and Regan are beginning to quarrel. Just as she is accusing him of loving Goneril, Goneril and Albany appear. Albany, fearing to lose his power, says that they must all fight together against the French. Edgar, still disguised, slips in and speaks to Albany while the others walk ahead. He gives the earl the letter he took from Oswald, but before Albany has time to read it, Edmund returns to say that the French army is in sight. The battle-hour has come.

A fatal letter

The British army defeats the French; Lear and Cordelia are captured. Cordelia asks to see her sisters, but Lear is happy to go straight to prison with her. Edmund sends them off to his castle, giving a letter to the captain of their guard.

> **Reunion**
> *I fear I am not in my perfect*
> *   mind.*
> *Methinks I should know*
> *   you and know this man;*
> *Yet I am doubtful: for I am*
> *   mainly ignorant*
> *What place this is, and all*
> *   the skill I have*
> *Remembers not these*
> *   garments; nor I know*
> *   not*
> *Where I did lodge last*
> *   night. Do not laugh at*
> *   me;*
> *For, as I am a man, I think*
> *   this lady*
> *To be my child Cordelia.*
>
> Act IV Sc vii

> **Happy in prison**
> *Come, let's away to prison;*
> *We two alone will sing like birds i' the cage:*
> *When thou dost ask me blessing, I'll kneel down,*
> *And ask of thee forgiveness: so we'll live,*
> *And pray, and sing, and tell old tales, and laugh*
> *At gilded butterflies, and hear poor rogues*
> *Talk of court news.*
>
> Act v Sc iii

Albany has now read Oswald's letter. He arrests Edmund as a traitor, and challenges him to fight one of his knights. Regan collapses. Goneril is not surprised, because she has poisoned her sister.

Edgar, in another guise, volunteers to fight against Edmund, and beats him in combat. Goneril rushes to his aid, but runs away when Albany threatens to reveal the letter's

contents. As Edmund grows weaker, Edgar admits his true identity. He is now Earl of Gloucester – his father has died of grief at the news that Lear is captured.

The news comes that Regan has died of the poison and Goneril has killed herself. Edmund, with his dying breath, sends Edgar to the castle – to stop the death-warrant he sent for Lear and Cordelia.

But Cordelia has already been executed, and Lear is crazed with grief. He killed her hangman, but could not save her. He dies weeping over her body.

Cordelia's death

No, no, no life!
Why should a dog, a horse,
*   a rat, have life,*
And thou no breath at all?
*   Thou'lt come no more,*
Never, never, never, never,
*   never!*
Pray you, undo this button:
*   thank you, sir.*
Do you see this? Look on
*   her, look, her lips,*
Look there, look there!

Act v Sc iii

Lear's grief

Howl, howl, howl, howl! O! you are men of stones:
Had I your tongues and eyes, I'd use them so
That heaven's vaults should crack. She's gone for ever.
I know when one is dead, and when one lives;
She's dead as earth. Lend me a looking-glass; If that her
breath will mist or stain the stone,
Why, then she lives.

Act v Sc iii

Characters in King Lear

Lear

Cordelia

love. He has lived with 'poor naked wretches', and thought, in his madness, about the falseness of human power and justice. He has learnt the hard way that those who speak the finest words, like Regan and Goneril, do not always have the finest feelings.

Cordelia

Lear's youngest daughter is truthful to a fault. She cannot flatter her father as her sisters do, and so loses her share of the kingdom. But the King of France realises that she is really the best of the three, and is happy to marry her. She is a courageous queen, able to lead an invading army to her father's rescue. When she discovers the full and sad truth about what has happened to Lear, she is appalled; she would treat even a dog better than that. Against Lear's rants about the basic cruelty of humans, we must place her sense of charity.

Regan

Regan seems less cruel to Lear at first – he goes to her when life at Goneril's court becomes impossible, thinking she will let him live as he wants. But she turns out as bad as her sister. She is physically even crueller, being willing to finish the blinding of Gloucester when the servants attack Cornwall.

Goneril

Lear's eldest daughter is cruel and vicious. She cannot bear being married to a good man like Albany, but prefers Edmund, as wicked as herself. Even when Lear is first living with her, she lets her servants ill-treat his beloved Fool. She has no loyalties at all, even poisoning her own sister when she becomes a rival for Edmund's love.

Regan

Goneril

Lear

The old king's trouble is that he wants the advantages of power even when he has given it up. He expects to be treated like a king even when he has nothing. But he learns from his terrible experiences. While once he required a hundred knights to hold his head up, by the end of the play he realises that all he needs in the world is Cordelia's

---

The sisters assess their father

Gon. *You see how full of changes his age is; the observation we have made of it hath not been little: he always loved our sister most; and with what poor judgment he hath now cast her off appears too grossly.*
Reg. *'Tis the infirmity of his age; yet he hath ever but slenderly known himself.*

Act I Sc i

Edgar

Edgar is a strange character. He is not quite all good, just as Edmund is not quite all bad; he is touchy, and a little devious. He obviously enjoys playing the madman, 'Poor Tom', and the chance this 'part' gives him to complain about the wicked ways of the world. He shows great sensitivity when he lets his blind father believe that he has been saved from death by a miracle. He is deeply moved by Lear's plight.

Edg. [Aside.] *My tears begin to take his part so much,*
They'll mar my counterfeiting. Act III Sc vi

Edgar

Edmund

Edmund

Thou, Nature, art my goddess; to thy law My services are bound.
Act I Sc ii

Edmund is a stage villain who knows no loyalty except to himself, but he has a tiny spark of goodness in him, which shows when he tries to save Lear and Cordelia from execution as he dies.

Kent

Gloucester

Gloucester

My duty cannot suffer To obey in all your daughters' hard commands:
Act III Sc iv

Gloucester, like Lear, is too easily taken in by flattery. He listens too readily to Edmund's lies about his brother, but when his character is tested he proves loyal and even brave, defying Cornwall and Regan even while they torture him.

The Fool

The Fool may be the wisest person in the play. A poor boy who lives by his wits (and his wit), he cannot afford the pride shown by his betters, such as Lear and Cordelia. His way of looking at the world is strangely twisted, but he sees how foolish Lear has been (and tells him so) before anyone else.

Fool

Kent

The Earl of Kent is a fiery, quarrelsome spirit. Like Edgar, he enjoys the chance to show his inner self through disguise. His loyalty to Lear and Cordelia survives even banishment, and he is a vital link between the two when Cordelia is in France.

The Fool's song

He that has a little tiny wit,
With hey, ho, the wind and the rain,
Must make content with his fortunes fit,
Though the rain it raineth every day.
Act III Sc ii

OTHELLO

Illustrations by Jonathon Heap

The story of Othello

Late one night in the city of Venice, two men approach the house of Senator Brabantio. Iago, a soldier, and Roderigo, a vain young gentleman, rouse the old man with shouts. 'Look to your house, your daughter and your bags! Thieves! Thieves!'.

At his window, the senator tells them to stop their drunken noise. He has refused to let Roderigo marry his daughter, Desdemona, and will not change his mind. Iago says they have bad news: Desdemona has eloped with his general, Othello, a Moor who serves the city for pay.

Iago has a reason for telling Brabantio. He is bitter because Othello has chosen Cassio as his lieutenant, giving Iago the lower rank of 'ancient' or ensign.

But for now, Iago must seem loyal. He goes to warn Othello that Brabantio is coming. Othello is not worried: the

> **Iago's false face**
> *Though I do hate him as I do hell-pains,*
> *Yet, for necessity of present life,*
> *I must show out a flag and sign of love,*
> *Which is indeed but sign.*
>
>
>
> Act I Sci

> **Othello calms Brabantio**
> *Keep up your bright swords,*
> *for the dew will rust*
> *them.*
> *Good signior, you shall*
> *more command with*
> *years*
> *Than with your weapons.*
>
> Act I Scii

Duke of Venice will not arrest his best general over such a trifle. Cassio arrives to summon Othello to the Duke's council chamber; after him comes Brabantio, with Roderigo and some soldiers.

Witchcraft

Brabantio draws his sword, but Othello softly refuses his challenge. The old man accuses him of bewitching Desdemona, and threatens to arrest him for sorcery. (He cannot believe she could simply fall in love with a black man.) But Othello points out that they are wanted by the Duke. Brabantio is glad to go, expecting the Duke to support him.

A threat to Venice

But the Duke has other things on his mind. A Turkish invasion fleet is sailing towards the island of Cyprus, which belongs to the Venetians.

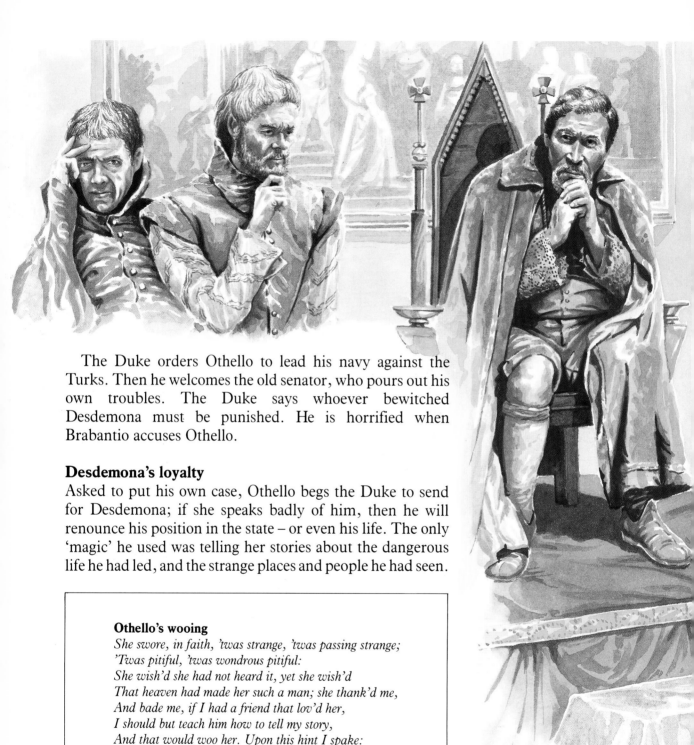

The Duke orders Othello to lead his navy against the Turks. Then he welcomes the old senator, who pours out his own troubles. The Duke says whoever bewitched Desdemona must be punished. He is horrified when Brabantio accuses Othello.

Desdemona's loyalty

Asked to put his own case, Othello begs the Duke to send for Desdemona; if she speaks badly of him, then he will renounce his position in the state – or even his life. The only 'magic' he used was telling her stories about the dangerous life he had led, and the strange places and people he had seen.

Othello's wooing

She swore, in faith, 'twas strange, 'twas passing strange;
'Twas pitiful, 'twas wondrous pitiful:
She wish'd she had not heard it, yet she wish'd
That heaven had made her such a man; she thank'd me,
And bade me, if I had a friend that lov'd her,
I should but teach him how to tell my story,
And that would woo her. Upon this hint I spake:
She lov'd me for the dangers I had pass'd,
And I lov'd her that she did pity them.
This only is the witchcraft I have us'd:

Act I Sciii

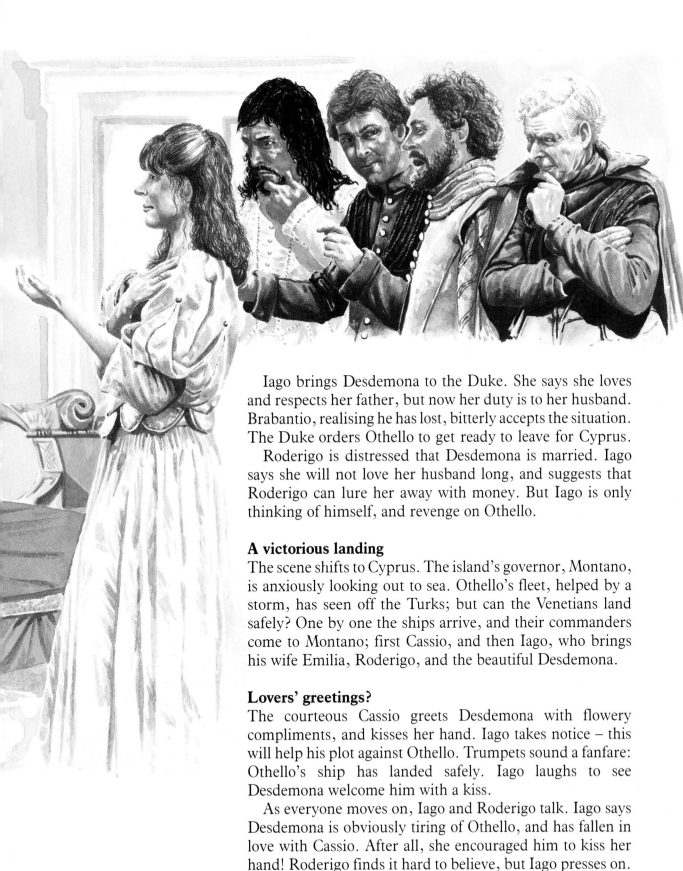

Iago brings Desdemona to the Duke. She says she loves and respects her father, but now her duty is to her husband. Brabantio, realising he has lost, bitterly accepts the situation. The Duke orders Othello to get ready to leave for Cyprus.

Roderigo is distressed that Desdemona is married. Iago says she will not love her husband long, and suggests that Roderigo can lure her away with money. But Iago is only thinking of himself, and revenge on Othello.

A victorious landing

The scene shifts to Cyprus. The island's governor, Montano, is anxiously looking out to sea. Othello's fleet, helped by a storm, has seen off the Turks; but can the Venetians land safely? One by one the ships arrive, and their commanders come to Montano; first Cassio, and then Iago, who brings his wife Emilia, Roderigo, and the beautiful Desdemona.

Lovers' greetings?

The courteous Cassio greets Desdemona with flowery compliments, and kisses her hand. Iago takes notice – this will help his plot against Othello. Trumpets sound a fanfare: Othello's ship has landed safely. Iago laughs to see Desdemona welcome him with a kiss.

As everyone moves on, Iago and Roderigo talk. Iago says Desdemona is obviously tiring of Othello, and has fallen in love with Cassio. After all, she encouraged him to kiss her hand! Roderigo finds it hard to believe, but Iago presses on.

He suggests Roderigo get Cassio into trouble by starting a fight with him. With Cassio out of the way, perhaps Desdemona will fall for him.

A devious plot

On his own, Iago reveals his plan for revenge. He will drive Othello mad with jealousy.

Iago's chance comes that night. He and Cassio are waiting to go on guard, during a festival to celebrate Othello's wedding and his victory. At first, Cassio refuses a drink – he has a weak head. But soon Iago has everyone singing drinking songs. Cassio forgets his resolution, and drinks along with the rest – just as Iago planned.

Cassio's disgrace

The drunken lieutenant staggers off. Iago sends Roderigo after him. Soon he returns at the point of Cassio's sword. Montano tries to part them, but Cassio fights him off. Othello, roused by the noise, is disgusted to see his lieutenant in such a state – and fighting with the governor of Cyprus!

Iago pretends to be reluctant to accuse Cassio, but his account is all the more damning for that. Othello believes every word. 'Cassio, I love thee,' he says, 'But never more be officer of mine.'

Poisoned advice

Cassio, sobering up, asks Iago for advice. Iago suggests he ask Desdemona to plead his case; Othello will refuse her nothing. (Perhaps he will also wonder why she is so keen to have Cassio reinstated, thinks Iago.) Next morning Cassio comes to Iago's house and easily charms Emilia into talking to Desdemona on his behalf.

As soon as she is asked, Desdemona promises to help. Othello and Iago appear, and Cassio hastily leaves. (Once again, he plays into Iago's hands.) 'Was not that Cassio parted from my wife?' asks Othello. Iago says it cannot be – 'No, sure, I cannot think it, that he would steal away so guilty-like, seeing you coming.' Iago's 'defence' shows Cassio in the worst possible light.

Innocent Desdemona at once begs her husband to forgive Cassio. 'Not now, sweet Desdemona; some other time', he says, but she persists. At last Othello wavers a little; Desdemona, satisfied for now, leaves him, and Iago sets to work to raise suspicion. He suggests that Othello should keep

Iago's song persuades Cassio to drink

And let me the canakin clink, clink;
And let me the canakin clink:
   A soldier's man;
   A life's but a span;
Why then let a soldier drink.   Act II Sc iii

a watch on his wife and Cassio. He goes, leaving Othello in terrible distress.

The fatal handkerchief

Desdemona and Emilia return. As soon as Othello sees his wife, he cries out, unable to believe she is untrue to him. She rushes to his side and asks if he is ill. He says he has a headache, and she tries to bandage his head with her embroidered handkerchief – but it is too small and she lets it drop to the ground.

As they leave, Emilia picks up the handkerchief. Iago has asked her to get it for him, and he is pleased to get his hands on it. His plan is to hide it in Cassio's house.

Othello returns, unable to decide what to think. He cannot bear the uncertainty, and must have proof of his wife's unfaithfulness. Iago says he saw Cassio wipe his beard with Desdemona's handkerchief. The horrified general orders Iago to kill Cassio. Iago says it will be done – 'but let her live'. In this way, he puts the most terrible idea of all into Othello's mind.

Othello wants to find out if Desdemona still has the handkerchief, which once belonged to his mother. He asks to borrow it, saying he has a cold; but of course she has not got it. He becomes angry when she denies losing it, and she makes it worse by trying to distract him by talking about Cassio. He leaves in a rage.

A woman scorned

Desdemona sadly tells Cassio that things are not going well; Othello is angry with her, and will not listen to her pleas. As she leaves, another woman comes to talk to Cassio – Bianca, a prostitute who is in love with him.

Bianca is upset because Cassio has not been to see her. He asks her to forgive him, then, astonishingly, gives her Desdemona's handkerchief. He has found it in his house, and likes the design; will Bianca sew him a copy? She naturally thinks another woman has given it to him, but she agrees to meet him later.

Othello loses control

Iago continues to torment Othello, who is now half-mad with jealousy, and completely in his power. He talks incoherently about honour, lust – and the handkerchief. At last he falls down into a fit.

> ### Desdemona promises her help
> *My lord shall never rest;*
> *I'll watch him tame, and talk him out of patience;*
> *His bed shall seem a school, his board a shrift;*
> *I'll intermingle every thing he does*
> *With Cassio's suit.*
> *Therefore be merry, Cassio;*
>
> Act III Sciii

> ### Jealousy stirs
> *O curse of marriage!*
> *That we can call these delicate creatures ours,*
> *And not their appetites. I had rather be a toad,*
> *And live upon the vapour of a dungeon,*
> *Than keep a corner in the thing I love*
> *For others' uses.*
>
> Act III Sciii

> ### Othello demands proof
> *By the world,*
> *I think my wife be honest and think she is not;*
> *I think that thou art just and think thou art not.*
> *I'll have some proof. Her name, that was as fresh*
> *As Dian's visage, is now begrim'd and black*
> *As mine own face. If there be cords or knives,*
> *Poison or fire or suffocating streams,*
> *I'll not endure it. Would I were satisfied!*
>
> Act III Sciii

While he is unconscious, Cassio comes, but Iago sends him away for a moment. Othello recovers; Iago tells him Cassio has been there, and suggests that he should listen to their conversation when he returns.

Mistaken conclusions
Iago and Cassio gossip about Bianca, mocking this pathetic woman. 'She gives it out that you shall marry her!' Cassio laughs at the very idea. But Othello thinks it is his wife they are discussing so crudely. Bianca herself arrives, thrusting Desdemona's handkerchief back into Cassio's hand. 'This is some minx's token!' Iago could not have hoped for better luck. Cassio runs off after Bianca.

Othello in the depths
Now Othello has murder on his mind. 'Get me some poison, Iago!' Iago says it would be better to strangle her on her marriage-bed. Othello agrees, but as they talk Desdemona

interrupts, bringing Lodovico, a Venetian gentleman with a letter from the Duke.

While he reads the letter, a summons back to Venice, Desdemona talks to Lodovico. Suddenly Othello turns round, shouts at her and hits her. Horrified, Lodovico asks if the letter has made him angry; but Iago hints that the general is mad.

At home, Othello questions Emilia about his wife's behaviour, and sends her to fetch Desdemona so that they can talk alone. He makes his terrible accusation to the poor, bewildered girl: 'Heaven truly knows that thou art false as hell.' The more she pleads innocence, the more angry he becomes.

Poor Desdemona confides in Emilia and Iago; she cannot see what she has done to provoke such jealousy. Emilia tries to console her.

Roderigo's jewels

As the ladies leave for supper, Roderigo confronts Iago. Iago had promised to win Desdemona for him, by giving her presents of jewels; now he is sick of waiting, and wants the jewels back. Of course, the jewels never reached her – Iago kept them for himself.

Iago retrieves this awkward situation by telling Roderigo that Othello has been recalled by the Duke. Only an unforeseen event, such as an 'accident' befalling Cassio might make him stay. Roderigo will have an opportunity to kill Cassio when he visits Bianca.

A duel in the street

Iago wants to get rid of both Cassio and Roderigo. He is still consumed with jealousy of the charming lieutenant, and he does not want to repay Roderigo for the presents he was supposed to have sent. He hopes that one will kill the other, and be hanged for murder.

He waits with Roderigo in the dark street. When Cassio appears, Roderigo stabs ineffectually at him. Cassio strikes back and wounds him. In the darkness, Iago stabs Cassio, who falls to the ground. Othello enters, thinking Iago has kept his promise to kill Cassio. He leaves to carry out his own dreadful plan.

Lodovico and his companion Gratiano arrive; Cassio revives and calls out for help – and so does Roderigo. In the confusion, Iago kills Roderigo.

The fatal handkerchief
*That handkerchief
Did an Egyptian to my
     mother give; . . .
. . . She dying gave it me;
And bid me, when my fate
     would have me wive,
To give it her. I did so: and
     take heed on't;
Make it a darling like your
     precious eye;
To lose't or give't away,
     were such perdition
As nothing else could
     match.*

Act III Sciv

Iago turns the screw
*Do but encave yourself,
And mark the fleers, the
     gibes, and notable
     scorns,
That dwell in every region
     of his face;
For I will make him tell the
     tale anew,
Where, how, how oft, how
     long ago, and when
He hath, and is again to
     cope your wife:
I say, but mark his gesture.*

Act IV Sci

Murderous thoughts
*Ay, let her rot, and perish,
and be damned to-night; for
she shall not live. No, my
heart is turned to stone; I
strike it, and it hurts my
hand. O! the world hath
not a sweeter creature; she
might lie by an emperor's
side and command him
tasks.*

Act IV Sci

Desdemona's last hour

Othello enters Desdemona's bedroom, determined that she shall die. When he sees her, he cannot bear to shed her blood, and kisses her for the last time; but he still believes that justice demands that she die. She wakes, and he asks if she has said her prayers.

Othello tells his wife to pray for forgiveness. When she asks him to explain, he accuses her of giving her handkerchief to Cassio. At last Desdemona realises that she and Cassio have been innocent victims of a plot – but the more she cries out, the more determined Othello becomes. She begs piteously for time – a day, half an hour, time to say a prayer; but Othello smothers her with a pillow.

Emilia rushes in. As she tells Othello the news of Roderigo's death, Desdemona cries out with her dying breath. 'O, who has done this deed?' asks Emilia. 'Nobody; I myself,' says Desdemona, and dies.

> ### The finality of death
> *Put out the light, and then put out the light:*
> *If I quench thee, thou flaming minister,*
> *I can again thy former light restore,*
> *Should I repent me; but once put out thy light,*
> *Thou cunning'st pattern of excelling nature,*
> *I know not where is that Promethean heat*
> *That can thy light relume.*
>
> Act v Sc ii

The truth comes out

Emilia turns on Othello in anger and distress. He confesses that he killed Desdemona, explaining that Iago had proved she was false. Emilia shouts at him in contempt, and calls for help. Montano, Iago and others come running. Iago says he only told Othello what he believed to be true. As the accusations fly, Othello mentions the handkerchief. Emilia, realising what has been going on, tells him she took the handkerchief and gave it to Iago.

Iago attacks his wife, who has such damning evidence against him, and kills her. He escapes, but Montano and his men run after him and arrest him.

At last Othello knows the dreadful truth. He finds his favourite sword, and stabs Iago, but is prevented from killing him. While the others untangle the whole story, he is lost in thought. Lodovico arrests him for the murder of Desdemona, and he asks to speak.

A final kiss

Othello asks that the others 'speak of me as I am'; they must not try to excuse what he has done, or make him out to be a terrible villain. Then he talks of a long-ago battle, when he killed a Turk; as he speaks of stabbing his enemy, he stabs himself. He falls on the bed beside the lifeless Desdemona, and dies kissing her.

> ### Othello's last words
> *When you shall these unlucky deeds relate,*
> *Speak of me as I am; nothing extenuate,*
> *Nor set down aught in malice: then, must you speak*
> *Of one that lov'd not wisely but too well;*
>
>
>
> Act v Scii

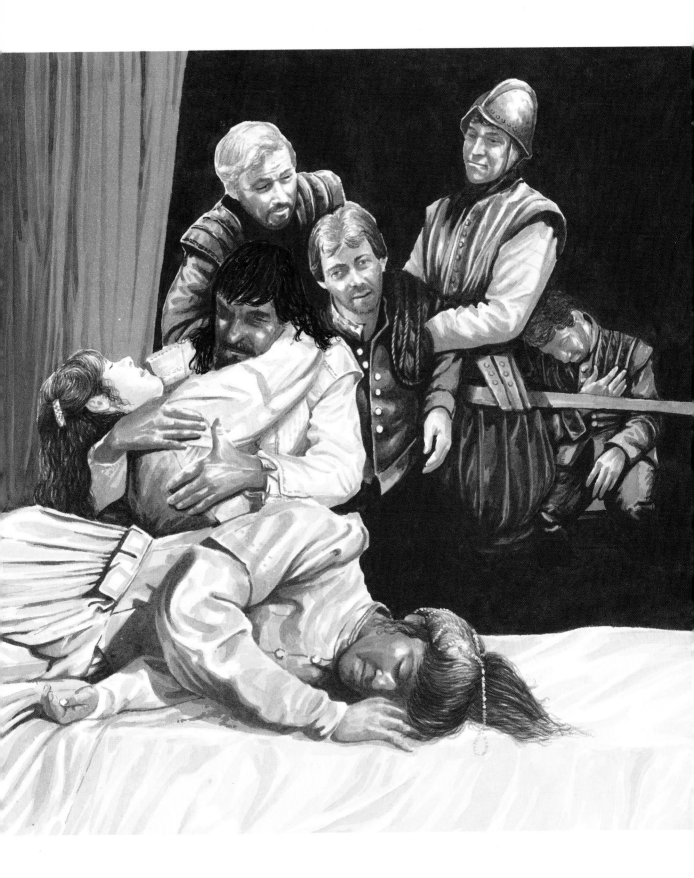

Characters in Othello

Othello

Othello

*O! now, for ever
Farewell the tranquil mind;
    farewell content!*

Act III Sciii

When we first meet Othello we cannot help but be impressed by his dignity and good sense. With gentle humour, he prevents a fight, calming the angry Brabantio without ridiculing him. At the Duke's council meeting, we learn something of his adventurous past. He is evidently a soldier worthy of the Duke's trust. In Cyprus, he shows his dislike of uncontrolled behaviour when he dismisses Cassio for a drunken brawl. But, when his own feelings are in question, he too easily loses control of himself. Iago plays quite cruelly on his deepest insecurities, especially the fear that, as a foreigner and a simple soldier, the sophisticated Venetians will laugh at him. He loves Desdemona so much that he cannot bear to lose her – and once the seeds of suspicion are sown, the terror turns into rage and he becomes literally mad with jealousy. Once Emilia has spoken, and revealed Iago's lies for what they are, he quickly sees how he has been deceived. But Desdemona is dead, and it is too late; Othello's only solution is to die himself.

Iago's view of Othello

*The Moor is of a free and open nature,
That thinks men honest that but seem to be so,
And will as tenderly be led by the nose
As asses are.*

Act I Sciii

Desdemona

*If I do vow a friendship,
    I'll perform it
To the last article;*

Act III Sciii

Desdemona shows herself when she first appears as a brave young woman. Having heard so much about the wars from Othello, she wants to see them for herself, and insists on coming to Cyprus with the army. But once she is there, safely married to the man she loves, she never thinks that anything could go wrong until it is too late. She does not know, as we do, how Iago is twisting Othello's feelings, but she is tactless when she insists on pressing Cassio's case when Othello obviously does not want to listen. As he becomes more and more angry with her, she simply cannot understand what is happening. Yet she remains loyal to the end, bravely hiding her feelings when the Venetian lords arrive to summon Othello home, and even, with her dying breath, trying to take all the blame herself.

Iago

Iago is a typical villain of Jacobean drama – a cold, cunning type who presents a false face to the world. He is known to the world as 'honest Iago', ever-ready with good advice, a drink or a joke. But under this cover he robs

Iago

Desdemona

Iago's philosophy

. . . not I for love and duty,
But seeming so, for my
peculiar end: Act I Sci

Roderigo, plots the downfall of Cassio, and deliberately drives Othello to murder to punish him for promoting Cassio instead of himself. He is quick to spot others' weaknesses – Cassio's weak head for liquor, as well as Othello's insecurity. He has an eye for jealousy especially, because he is himself both envious and jealous.

People fatally trust him because he seems an unsophisticated man of action, yet underneath he is highly intelligent, able to make devious plans and change them quickly to take advantage of any new situation. He might have made a good general himself, if only he had turned his mind away from his own advantage.

tries to get Othello to forgive him his disgrace in the proper courtly manner, sending messages through Desdemona, but Othello, under Iago's influence, also mistakes his fine manners for something darker.

Emilia

I care not for thy sword;
I'll make thee known,
Though I lost twenty lives.

Act v Scii

Emilia really is 'honest' – she speaks her mind freely, and nothing will stop her revealing the truth about the handkerchief at the end. She is kind and reassuring to Desdemona when her mistress is in the depths of misery. But, like Desdemona, she does not see what is going on under her nose. When she finds the handkerchief, she never asks why Iago should want such a thing, but simply takes it to please him. Though she must know her husband better than anyone, she does not recognise him for the villain he is until his plans have reached their tragic conclusion.

Cassio

A typical Renaissance courtier, Cassio is charming, intelligent and capable. He and Iago do not understand each other. He is puzzled by Iago's crude humour. Iago sees his courtly treatment of Desdemona and Emilia as lustful advances. He

Cassio

Iago's view of Cassio

Cassio's a proper man; . . .
. . . He hath a person and a smooth dispose
To be suspected; framed to make women false.

Act I Sciii

Emilia

The life and plays of Shakespeare

Life of Shakespeare

1564 William Shakespeare born at Stratford-upon-Avon.

1582 Shakespeare marries Anne Hathaway, eight years his senior.

1583 Shakespeare's daughter, Susanna, is born.

1585 The twins, Hamnet and Judith, are born.

1587 Shakespeare goes to London.

1591-2 Shakespeare writes *The Comedy of Errors*. He is becoming well-known as an actor and writer.

1592 Theatres closed because of plague.

1593-4 Shakespeare writes *Titus Andronicus* and *The Taming of the Shrew*: he is member of the theatrical company, the Chamberlain's Men.

1594-5 Shakespeare writes *Romeo and Juliet*.

1595 Shakespeare writes *A Midsummer Night's Dream*.

1595-6 Shakespeare writes *Richard II*.

1596 Shakespeare's son, Hamnet, dies. He writes *King John* and *The Merchant of Venice*.

1597 Shakespeare buys New Place in Stratford.

1597-8 Shakespeare writes *Henry IV*.

1599 Shakespeare's theatre company opens the Globe Theatre.

1599-1600 Shakespeare writes *As You Like It*, *Henry V* and *Twelfth Night*.

1600-01 Shakespeare writes *Hamlet*.

1602-03 Shakespeare writes *All's Well That Ends Well*.

1603 Elizabeth I dies. James I becomes king. Theatres closed because of plague.

1603-04 Shakespeare writes *Othello*.

1605 Theatres closed because of plague.

1605-06 Shakespeare writes *Macbeth* and *King Lear*.

1606-07 Shakespeare writes *Antony and Cleopatra*.

1607 Susanna Shakespeare marries Dr John Hall. Theatres closed because of plague.

1608 Shakespeare's granddaughter, Elizabeth Hall, is born.

1609 *Sonnets* published. Theatres closed because of plague.

1610 Theatres closed because of plague. Shakespeare gives up his London lodgings and retires to Stratford.

1611-12 Shakespeare writes *The Tempest*.

1613 Globe Theatre burns to the ground during a performance of *Henry VIII*.

1616 Shakespeare dies on 23 April.

Shakespeare's plays

Love's Labour's Lost
The Comedy of Errors
The Two Gentlemen of Verona
Henry VI Part 1
Henry VI Part 2
Henry VI Part 3
Richard III
Romeo and Juliet
Titus Andronicus
Richard II
A Midsummer Night's Dream

King John
The Merchant of Venice
The Taming of the Shrew
Henry IV Part 1
Henry IV Part 2
Henry V
The Merry Wives of Windsor
Much Ado About Nothing
Julius Caesar
As You Like It
Twelfth Night
All's Well That Ends Well
Troilus and Cressida

Hamlet
Measure for Measure
Othello
King Lear
Macbeth
Antony and Cleopatra
Coriolanus
Timon of Athens
Pericles
Cymbeline
The Winter's Tale
The Tempest
Henry VIII

Index

Major characters are indexed only to their first appearance and description. Minor characters have all their page references.

Adam 40, 41
Aguecheek, Sir Andrew 54
  character of 66
Albany, Duke of 130, 138
Angus 98, 99
Antonio (*Merchant of Venice*) 26
  character of 35
  quotes: his sadness 26; on his fate 32
Antonio (*Twelfth Night*) 56, 62
Arden, Mary 6
Artemidorus 87
As You Like It: the characters 50–52
  story of 39–49; Oliver plots against his brother 39; the banished Duke 39; the wrestling match 39; Rosalind is banished 39; in the Forest of Arden 40; at the old Duke's encampment 41; in praise of Rosalind 42; the jester in love 42; 'the proud disdainful shepherdess' 44; the wooing of Rosalind 44; enter Oliver 45; Audrey's suitor dismissed 46; love at first sight 46; a joyful day 47; Rosalind's promises 47; the promises fulfilled 49; Rosalind's epilogue 49
At the break of day (quote) 74
Audrey 42
  character of 52

Banquo 98
  character of 112
Bassanio 26
  character of 36
  quote: on his friend's high spirits 28
Belch, Sir Toby 54
  character of 66
  quote: urging Sir Andrew to dance 55
Benvolio 68, 69, 70, 72
Bianca 150, 151
Bottom 13
  character of 24
  quote: his instructions to the fairies 24
Brabantio, Senator 144, 146, 147
Brutus 85
  character of 95
  quotes: bids farewell to Cassius 93; his farewell to his followers 93; his idea of honour 95; on the need for action 90; why the conspirators need him 85
Burgundy, Duke of 128

Calphurnia 87
Capulet, Lady 69
  character of 81
  quote: describes Paris 70
Capulet, Lord 68
  character of 81
  quotes: his threat 75; on Juliet's death 76
Casca 85, 87
Caskets, quotes: the golden casket's message 30; the inscriptions on 30
Cassio 144
  character of 157

quote: greets Desdemona 148
Cassius 85
  character of 96
  despairs 93
Celia 39
  character of 51
  quote: a close friendship 51
Charles 39
Cinna 87
Claudius 114
  character of 126
  quote: his love for Gertrude 126
Cobweb 16
Cordelia 128
  character of 141
  quotes: her death 140; her kindness 137; her love (quote) 128
Corin 40
Cornwall, Duke of 131, 132, 134, 136
  quote: his cruelty 134
Country life, quote: the pleasures of 40
Country song, a (quote) 41

Decius 87
Demetrius 12
  character of 23
Desdemona 144
  character of 156
  quotes: her plea 148; promises her help 150
Disorder in the stars (quote) 131
Disturbed night, a (quote) 102
Donalbain 103
Drayton, Michael 9
Duke, old 39, 40, 41, 49
Duke of Venice (*Merchant of Venice*) 32, 33
Duke of Venice (*Othello*) 144, 146, 147
Duncan 99
  character of 112
  quote: describes Macbeth's castle 100

Edgar 131
  character of 142
  quote: a fearful precipice 136
Edmund 128
  character of 142
Egeus 12, 19
Emilia 147
  character of 157
Escalius, Prince of Verona 68, 72, 78, 80
  quotes: blames the Capulets and Montagues 80; on the story of Romeo and Juliet 80

Fabian 60, 62
Fairies, quotes: blessing 20; song (quote) 15
Feste, the Clown 55
  character of 66
  quotes: his love song 57; his song 64
Fleance 104
Flute 13, 20
Fool, the 131
  character of 142
  quotes: can't win 131; his song 142
Fortinbras 124
France, King of 128, 132
Frederick, Duke 39, 42, 49

Gertrude 114
  character of 126
Ghost 114, 115

Gloucester, Earl of 128
  character of 142
Gobbo, Lancelot 27
Goneril 128
  character of 141
  quotes: assessment of Lear 141; her complaints 131
Gratiano (*Merchant of Venice*) 28, 31, 33
Gratiano (*Othello*) 152
Guildenstern 116

Hamlet: the characters 125–126
  story of 114–124; the new King of Denmark 114; a ghostly meeting 114; Hamlet feigns madness 116; Hamlet's plot to trick the King 116; Hamlet spurns Ophelia 116; the play's the thing 119; a chance to kill the King 119; Polonius behind the arras 120; Ophelia's madness 120; Claudius urges Laertes to revenge 122; the death of Ophelia 122; at the graveyard 122; the fatal duel 124; Hamlet's death 124
Hamlet 114
  character of 125
  quotes: his instructions to the players 119; his melancholy 116; his thoughts on revenge 119; longing for death 114; on life and death 117; rejects Ophelia 118; remembers Yorick 123
Hathaway, Anne 7
Helena 12
  character of 23
Hermia 12
  character of 23
  quote: description of 12
Hippolyta 12
  character of 22
Horatio 114, 115, 122, 124
  quote: his farewell 124
How many knights? (quote) 132

Iago 144
  character of 156
  quotes: his false face 144; his philosophy 157; his song persuades Cassio to drink 149; his view of Cassio 157; his view of Othello 156; turns the screw 152

Jaques 41
  character of 52
  quotes: his melancholy 52; on the seven ages of man 42
Jessica 28
  character of 36
Jonson, Ben 9
Juliet 69
  character of 81
  quotes: declares her love 71; her farewell 74; her parting words 71; longs for nightfall 73; on Romeo's name 70
Julius Caesar: the characters 95–96
  story of 84–94; Caesar for emperor? 85; dangerous Cassius 85; a conspiracy is born 85; Brutus is troubled 85; introducing the conspirators 87; Portia's pleas 87; Calphurnia's dream 87; the death of Caesar 87; Caesar's funeral 89; civil war

and discord 90; enter the ghost of Caesar 91; on the plains of Philippi 92; Brutus and Cassius exchange farewells 92; Cassius's defeat 92; the death of Cassius 92; Brutus finds his comrades dead 92; enter the victors 94
Julius Caesar 84
  character of 95
  quotes: death 88; describes Cassius 96; his ambition 85; his comments on Cassius 85; on death 87

Kent, Earl of 128
  character of 142
  quote: insults the villainous Oswald 132
King Lear: the characters 141–142
  story of 128–140; words of love 128; a wicked son 128; Kent's loyalty 130; the Fool 131; Edmund's plot 131; Lear dispossessed 132; the blasted heath 132; Gloucester in exile 134; a strange new friend 134; Gloucester is blinded 134; a faithless wife 136; summons to arms 136; a leap in the dark 136; miraculous rescue? 136; mad Lear 137 Lear and Cordelia reunited 138; a fatal letter 138

Laertes 114, 120, 122, 124
Laurence, Friar 72
  character of 82
  quotes: his advice to the Capulets 77; his warning 72
Lear, King 128
  character of 141
  quotes: defies the storm 133; his grief 140; his newfound compassion 134; hopes for happiness in prison 138; reunion with Cordelia 138
Lennox 103
Lepidus 90
Lodovico 152
Lorenzo 28
  character of 36
  quotes: declares his love for Jessica 29; on the power of music 34
Love song, a (quote) 47
Lucius 86
Lucy, Sir Thomas 7
Lysander 12
  character of 23

Macbeth 8
  the characters 110–112
  story of 98–109; meeting the witches 98; how brave Macbeth defeats the enemy 98; Macbeth and Banquo meet the witches 98; Macbeth dreams of becoming king 99; Macbeth is honoured with the King's visit 99; Lady Macbeth plans a murder 99; Macbeth has his fears and doubts 100; Lady Macbeth's anger 101; Macbeth sees a blood-stained dagger 101; how Macbeth murders Duncan 101; the horrible deed is discovered 103; Macbeth becomes King of Scotland 103; the new King plans another murder 104;

Macbeth does not confide in
the Queen 104; what happens
at the banquet 104; the
witches foretell disaster 105;
Macbeth's revenge on
Macduff 106; Malcolm tests
Macduff's loyalty 106; Lady
Macbeth sleepwalks 106;
Macbeth prepares for battle
108; when Birnam wood
meets Dunsinane 108
Macbeth 98
 character of 110
 quotes: for whom there is no
 going back 104; his ambitions
 111; his vision of a dagger
 101; no comfortable old age
 for 111; on how meaningless
 life is 108; on sleep 103; on
 the murder of Duncan 111;
 summoned to Duncan's
 murder 101
Macbeth, Lady 99
 character 111
 quotes: dismisses failure 111;
 her accusation of cowardice
 110; her determination to kill
 Duncan 100; on Macbeth's
 nature 99; sleepwalking 108
Macduff 103
 character of 112
 quote: his description of
 Macbeth 110
Malcolm 99, 103, 106, 108
Malvolio 54
 character of 65
 quote: what he reads 60
Maria 54, 55, 56, 57, 60
Mark Antony 85
 character of 96
 quotes: his funeral oration 90;
 his lament 89; his tribute to
 Brutus 94
Merchant of Venice, The:
 the characters 35-36
 story of 26-34; Bassanio's
 problems 26; Portia and her
 suitors 26; Shylock strikes a
 bargain 26; an exotic suitor
 for Portia 27; a clown leaves
 his master 27; introducing
 Shylock's daughter, Jessica 28;
 exit Jessica with the jewels 28;
 Morocco chooses the casket
 29; Bassanio makes his way to
 Belmont 30; disastrous news
 in Venice 30; Bassanio
 chooses a casket 31; news of
 Antonio 31; in the Venetian
 courtroom 32; enter the
 young 'doctor of law' 32; how
 Shylock is defeated 33; a gift
 for the lawyer 33; harmony -
 and disharmony - in Belmont
 34
Mercutio 69
 character of 82
Metellus 87
Midsummer Night's Dream, A:
 the characters 22-24;
 story of 2-21: a royal wedding
 12; lovers' difficulties 12; a
 plan to run away 12; how
 Helena betrays her friend 12;
 the tradesmen and their play
 13; quarrel of Titania and
 Oberon 14; the love potion
 14; Puck's mistake 15; a
 terrible mix-up 16; Bottom
 turned into an ass 16; Titania
 in love with an ass 16;
 Oberon's plan to sort out the

mix-up 17; more
 complications 18; Hermia and
 Helena quarrel 18; Oberon
 makes it better again 18;
 Titania spellbound 19;
 Oberon and Titania
 reconciled 19; what the
 hunters find 19; recounting
 the events of the midsummer
 night 19; Bottom
 untransformed 20; the
 'tragedy' of Pyramus and
 Thisbe 20; the fairies' blessing
 20
Montague, Lord 78, 80
Montano 147, 148, 154
Morocco, Prince of 27
 quote: his appeal to Portia 27
Moth 16
Mustard Seed 16

Nerissa 26, 31, 34
Nurse, the 69
 character of 82

Oberon 14
 character of 22-23
Octavius 90, 92, 94
Oliver 39
 character of 51
Olivia 55
 character of 65
 quotes: criticises Malvolio 65;
 leads Sebastian to the priest
 62; on her beauty 55
Ophelia 116
 character of 125
 quotes: her cry of despair 126;
 her death 122; her lament
 120; her madness 120; on
 Hamlet's nature 125
Orlando 39
 character of 50
 quote: before the wrestling
 match 39; expresses his
 gratitude 40
Orsino, Duke 55
 character of 65
 quotes: calls for music 58; his
 advice 58; on love 54; on the
 sufferings of love 58
Oswald 130, 131
Othello: the characters 156-157
 story of 144-155; witchcraft
 144; a threat to Venice 144;
 Desdemona's loyalty 146; a
 victorious landing 147; lovers'
 greetings? 147; a devious plot
 148; Cassio's disgrace 148;
 poisoned advice 148; the fatal
 handkerchief 150; a woman
 scorned 150; Othello loses
 control 150; mistaken
 conclusions 151; Othello in
 the depths 151; Roderigo's
 jewels 152; a duel in the street
 152; Desdemona's last hour
 153, the truth comes out 154;
 a final kiss 154
Othello 144
 character of 156
 quotes: calms Brabantio 144;
 demands proof 150; his last
 words 154; his wooing 146;
 jealousy stirs 150; murderous
 thoughts 152; on the fatal
 handkerchief 152; on the
 finality of death 154

Paris 68
 character of 82
Pease Blossom 16

Phebe 40, 44, 45, 46, 49
Pindarus 92
Polonius 116
 character of 125
 quote: his advice to his son
 114
Portia (Julius Caesar) 87
 character of 96
 quotes: a noble Roman
 woman 87; chides Brutus
 86
Portia (Merchant of Venice) 26
 character of 35
 quotes: describes one suitor
 26; her acceptance 31; her
 plea for mercy 32
Puck 14
 character of 24
 quote: his epilogue 21

Queen Mab's carriage (quote)
 70
Quince 13, 20

Regan 128
 character of 141
 quote: assessment of Lear 141
Richard III 8
Roderigo 144, 147, 152
Romeo and Juliet 8
 the characters 81-82
 story of 68-80; a street battle
 68; the love-sick Romeo 68; a
 proposal of marriage 68; why
 Romeo goes to the ball 68;
 Juliet hears of the marriage
 proposal 69; Romeo and his
 friends go to the ball 69;
 Romeo meets Juliet 69; Juliet
 on the balcony 70; Romeo
 and Juliet declare their love
 70; Romeo arranges the
 marriage 72; the marriage
 ceremony 72; a fatal duel
 takes place 72; Romeo gets his
 revenge 72; Juliet learns of
 Romeo's banishment 73; Lord
 Capulet arranges a marriage
 73; Romeo and Juliet's
 farewell 74; Juliet refuses to
 marry Paris 74; the Friar's
 plan to stop the marriage 75;
 the wedding preparations 76;
 Juliet is frightened 76; how
 Juliet is found dead 76; what
 happens to Romeo in Mantua
 77; how the Friar's plan goes
 awry 77; Romeo and Paris
 meet at Juliet's tomb 77; the
 death of Romeo 78; Juliet
 awakes 78; the bodies are
 discovered 78; the Friar
 explains the tragedy 80; the
 story is confirmed by Romeo's
 servant 80; the Montagues
 and Capulets are reconciled
 80
Romeo 68
 character of 81
 quotes: gazes on Juliet 78; his
 dream in Mantua 77; his
 farewell 74; his last kiss 78; on
 seeing Juliet on the balcony
 70; on the nature of love 68;
 swears his love 71
Rosalind 39
 character of 50
 quotes: her rebuke 44; her
 views on love 42; in love 50;
 love explained 46; to die for
 love? 45; what love is 46; why
 she must leave 40

Rosencrantz 116
Ross 98, 99

Shakespeare, Hamnet 7
Shakespeare, John 6
Shakespeare, Judith 7
Shakespeare, Susanna 7, 9
Shakespeare, William 6-9
 his life and plays 158
Shylock 26
 character of 35
 quotes: his instructions to
 Jessica 28; his reason for
 revenge 30
Silvius 40, 44, 45, 46, 49
Snout 13, 20
Snug 13, 20
Sonnets 8
 'dark lady' of 8
Southampton, Earl of 8, 8
Starveling 13, 20
Stratford-upon-Avon 6-7, 6, 7, 9
Strato 94

Taming of the Shrew, The 8
Theseus 12
 character of 22
Titania 14
 character of 22-23
 quotes: instructions to her
 fairies 17; where she sleeps
 15; with Bottom 19
Titinius 92
Topas, Sir 62
Touchstone 40
 character of 52
 quotes: a fool's live 52; his
 dismissal of William 46; the
 courtier 49
Trebonius 87
Twelfth Night: the characters
 65-66
 story of 54-64; a shipwreck
 54; introducing Sir Toby
 Belch 54; Viola becomes the
 page Cesario 55; Olivia with
 her household 55; Sebastian is
 alive 56; a night of
 merrymaking 56; making a
 fool of Malvolio 57; Duke
 Orsino is lovesick 58; how
 Malvolio is tricked 60; a duel
 is planned 60; Malvolio's 'very
 strange manner' 60; Sebastian
 and Antonio in Illyria 60; how
 the duke is stopped 62; love at
 first sight 62; Sir Topas, the
 curate, visits Malvolio 62; a
 formal betrothal takes place
 62; mistaken identity 62; a
 double wedding is planned 63
Tybalt 69
 character of 82

Viola 54
 character of 65
 quotes: follows the Duke 63;
 how she would woo a lover
 56; on a woman's love 59

William 46
witches, three, quotes: their
 brew 106; their chant 99

Yorick 122